IT'S NOT A
TOMB
IT'S A
WOMB

BOB SORGE

OASIS
HOUSE

KANSAS CITY, MISSOURI

Editor: Edie Mourey
Cover design: Rob Williams

Stay connected with Bob at:
oasishouse.com
YouTube.com/bobsorge
Facebook.com/BobSorgeMinistry
Blog: bobsorge.com
Instagram: bob.sorge
Twitter.com/BOBSORGE

CONTENTS

1

CRUCIFIED

On the night of His betrayal—just hours before He would be crucified—Jesus endeavored to prepare His disciples for His excruciating death. He knew what was coming but they didn't. To help them process what they were about to witness, Jesus used a metaphor. In fact, He used metaphors frequently as a way for His message to penetrate more effectively.

Metaphors paint word pictures. The pictures play in front of our eyes like movies. We not only *hear* what's said, but we also *see* it.

To portray the intensity of His sufferings, Jesus used childbirth as a metaphor:

> A woman, when she is in labor, has sorrow because her hour has come; but as soon as she has given birth to the child, she no longer remembers the anguish, for joy that a human being has been born into the world (John 16:21).

The disciples didn't fully understand in that moment, but He was saying to them, "I'm pregnant."

What was Jesus pregnant with?

He was pregnant with Prophecy; He was pregnant with Purpose; He was pregnant with Possibility.

Things were about to get messy.

In essence, Jesus was alerting them, "I'm about to go into labor—into *hard* labor. You're going to be distracted with the anguish, the sorrow, the travail, the birth pangs, the contractions, the pushing."

At the cross, we're looking at God in labor; at the resurrection, we see the baby being born. The resurrection was the birthing of our salvation, of the new covenant, of the Church, of a new and living way into the Father's embrace. What joy—that now millions of children would be born into the kingdom of God!

Why was the labor so intense? Because it was a real big baby!

GOD'S PERSPECTIVE ON THE CROSS

In one sense, the cross was a huge setback—in the sense that our Champion died. But God has consistently proven throughout history that every advance in the kingdom is preceded by a setback. He views our setbacks differently than we do; He sees them from an eternal vantage point.

When the disciples looked at the cross, they saw everything shutting down; but when God looked at the cross, He saw everything opening up.

When the disciples looked at the cross, they saw the end of everything; when God looked at the cross, He saw a new beginning to everything.

When the disciples looked at the cross, all they could see was a massive setback; when God looked at the cross, He saw a massive setup.

When the disciples looked at the cross, they saw Jesus getting crushed in the heel; when God looked at the cross, He saw Satan getting crushed in the head (Gen 3:15).

When the disciples looked at the cross, all they could see was a tomb; when God looked at the cross, He saw a womb (John 16:21).

THE CONTRACTIONS BECOME FRIENDS

When a woman goes into labor, the contractions actually become her friends. They assure her that, after long months of anticipation and discomfort, the baby is finally going to come out. The birth pangs crash upon her being in waves of inescapable travail, and she knows the only way forward is to *push this thing out*. The pain helps her push.

When a woman goes into labor, her eyes change. Something comes over her, and she goes, "We're not staying here." A steely resolve comes upon her that nobody can soften. All the force of her soul focuses on one thing: *This must change.*

Everybody in the birthing room becomes her enemy. "Get out of my way. I've got some pushing to do."

The contractions become her friends to help her complete the task of pushing and birthing a new life into the world.

In a similar way, the nails became Jesus' friends.

Hanging on the cross, His eyes changed. Something inside Him went, "We're not staying here." The searing bolts of electricity that flashed from hands to feet placed Him in the inescapable stranglehold of childbirth. The pain became birth pangs that helped Him push.

"GIVE ME MY NAILS"

I hear Jesus saying from the cross, "Give Me My nails!"

"Give Me My nails—I've got something to birth here.

"Give Me My nails so I can stretch My arms even further to show you how much I love you.

"Give Me My nails so I can earn My stripes as the Captain of your salvation.

"Give Me My nails and I'll hammer out your redemption right here on this hill." (The Carpenter from Nazareth knew what to do with His nails.)

"Give Me My nails, and I'll nail every accusation the adversary uses against you.

"Give Me My nails, and I'll nail the requirements of the law to this cross."

Paul wrote about this in Colossians 2:14.

> Having wiped out the handwriting of requirements that was against us, which was contrary to us. And He has taken it out of the way, having nailed it to the cross.

Moses' law was laden with the requirements necessary to get close to God. To draw near to Him, we had to meet His standards of righteousness. The law contained a long list of dos and don'ts, and it produced a performance-based religion that was stifling and impossible to satisfy. No one could measure up. The requirements kept tripping us up, which is why Paul said they were "contrary to us." Jesus nailed those contrary requirements to the cross, wiped them out, and ushered us into the rich domain of grace.

Now, instead of laboring feverishly to attain a righteousness based upon our personal performance, we receive the righteousness of God based upon the heroic performance of Christ on the cross. Let me say it another way. When we place our faith in the cross of Christ, God by His grace credits to us Jesus' performance on the cross. By faith, we "become the righteousness of God" in Christ (2 Cor 5:21). The righteousness that God gives by grace through faith is arguably the most stunning benefit of Christ's cross.

Again, Jesus nailed the requirements of the law to the cross. When you look at the cross, your first impression is that they're nailing *Him*; but He's like, "I'm nailing *it*." It was The Great Reversal. When they nailed Him, He nailed it.

"Give Me My nails. I've got some pushing to do."

PAIN CAN BE A FRIEND

Pain can actually become your friend. "How so?" you might wonder. Because of the way it can move you. Pain can move you to take measures you would have never taken under normal circumstances. For example, pain can cause a parent to exert heroic effort to save an endangered child.

Pain can also become your friend in your spiritual life. Sometimes God uses pain to cause us to reach for things in the kingdom we would not have otherwise pursued. Just as hunger drives someone to work hard, fiery trials can produce spiritual hunger within us that makes us reach for the release of His power and purpose (Prov 16:26).

When pain moves you to new places in God, you'll come to see it as your friend.

Pain will take you on roads you would have never traveled. Pain will take you to places in God others wouldn't dare to venture. Pain will make you desperate to hear God's voice. Pain will help you change.

Some people haven't changed because they're not yet in enough pain.

Suffering will wash from you the fear of man and immerse you in the fear of the Lord. When you get in enough pain, you won't care about the opinions of people anymore. All you'll care about is the opinion of One.

In a sense, a woman in labor becomes grateful for the painful contractions because, after months of carrying her growing baby, the birth pangs announce, "Finally! Finally, this baby's coming out!" In gratefulness, a woman's response is like, "Let's do this! Bring it on!"

There are some things in the kingdom of God you'll never birth until you're in enough pain.

FIRSTBORN FROM THE DEAD

Scripture calls Jesus "the firstborn from the dead," which means that at His resurrection He was born from the dead (Col 1:18; Rev 1:5). As Acts 13:33 says, at the resurrection He was *begotten* of the Father. Never before had such a thing happened. Others—such as Lazarus—had been resurrected from the dead, but their resurrections were only temporary, and they eventually died again. Jesus' resurrection was different. He will never again die, as He said to John, "Behold, I am alive forevermore" (Rev 1:18). To describe this unprecedented resurrection, Scripture uses the words *born* and *begotten*. He was born from the dead, never to die again.

Furthermore, He was the *firstborn*. In other words, He was the first of *many* to be born from the dead. His resurrection cut a path for others to follow, including many who are reading this book. When you believe in His death and resurrection, you get on the same course He charted. Like Him you'll die, be buried, and then be born from the dead. He promised emphatically that He will raise you up on the last day, and you will never again die (John 6:40).

I'm going to tell you something about the firstborn that I didn't discover until I had children of my own. I have three children—Joel, Katie, and Michael—and at the time of this writing six grandchildren. The world's six *cutest* grandchildren!

Joel is my firstborn. He was born in the 1900s, way back in time when you didn't know the gender of your baby until they came out. I still remember that day vividly because it was such a holy, spiritual experience.

When the pangs of hard labor gripped my wife, her eyes changed. She became entirely focused on one thing: *pushing.* She pushed with every fiber of her soul and with every ounce of her strength. Hour after hour. Contraction upon contraction.

It seemed to me like she was trying to push a head the size of a soccer ball out of an opening the size of a pinhole. I looked at the undertaking and thought to myself, "Impossible. This will never happen."

Her battle to birth the baby was such a struggle that, as I stood before her and stared at the proceedings, I literally thought to myself, *I can't believe that seven billion people have come into the world like this!* It was just *that* intense.

Then, when my second child—Katie—was born, she just slid right out! I was stunned at how quickly she came out because I was anticipating an encore. We barely got set up in the birthing room and *whoosh*, it was over. That's when I learned something about the firstborn—theirs is often the most difficult delivery. Why? Because the firstborn is opening a birth canal for the first time.

Jesus Christ was the firstborn from the dead. As such, He opened the birth canal of resurrection for the first time. That was the hard one. He took on the big boys—death, hell, Satan, the grave—and rose victoriously over them all. Following His steps, we now have the privilege of passing through the same birth canal of resurrection and rising with a glorified body to be with Him forever.

Gratefully, our passage through the birth canal of resurrection is so much easier than His was. He did the heavy lifting for us. Even though we will pass through the same birth canal, it's going to be a lot easier for us because of the passageway He opened. We will still die, but the sting of death has been removed (1 Cor 15:55), and we'll rise together with our mighty Forerunner into eternal life.

This is the great hope of our Gospel. May all praise and honor be lifted to the name of our Lord Jesus Christ!

And yet, even though our passage through the birth canal is much easier than His, it still seems really intense to us. Why?

Because our capacity for enduring difficulty is so small. But here's the thing. Our participation with Jesus in His crucifixion, death, burial, and resurrection is incredibly dignifying for us. We have the honor of experiencing the same thing He experienced, even if it's at just a fraction of the intensity. Thus, our sufferings actually become our greatest dignity. By experiencing death and resurrection together with Him, our intimacy with Him takes on new realms of understanding, identification, and delight. He navigated the hardest part and now has given us the dignity of following His steps (1 Pet 2:21).

EPICENTER OF LABOR

I began this chapter quoting John 16:21, where Jesus indicated His labor on the cross was like childbirth. He was doing something from His belly. At first glance, we might suppose He was laboring on the cross from His hands and feet. But He tipped us off in John 16:21 that He was actually doing it from His spirit. He travailed with His spirit on the cross in order to birth our redemption.

I have found it helpful to identify the seat of the human spirit. In fact, I've found it helpful to identify the seat of a variety of functions within our being. Here are some of the places from which we operate:

- The seat of the human mind is the cranium.
- The seat of the human will is the neck. (Those who resisted the will of God in Scripture were sometimes called *stiff-necked*.)
- The seat of our convictions and values is our heart.
- The seat of our emotions and feelings is down in our lower intestinal or abdominal area.
- Somewhere between our feelings (intestines) and convictions (heart) is the seat of our spirit. It's in the

vicinity of our solar plexus. Jesus pointed to this when He said that the living waters of the Holy Spirit would flow out of our *belly* (John 7:38 KJV).

Locating my spirit's resting place helps me relate to God. Here's what I mean. When I want to activate my spirit and connect with the Holy Spirit, I don't find that my spirit gets activated by focusing on my mind, or even centering on my heart. When I want to engage my spirit, I go to my belly.

That's how Jesus did it. He labored on the cross *from His spirit so* He could bring to birth the purpose for which He came into the world.

Let's follow His example. When you find yourself in excruciating trouble, do your trial from your spirit. Your fiery trial is an indicator that God has impregnated you with something deep on the inside. Grow the good thing He's placed within you, bring it to full term, and then *push*. God wants to birth something through your life that will enrich many others around you. A generation will be strengthened to believe God for great things because of the way you endured in faith.

THE HOLY SPIRIT LABORS

On the cross, Jesus groaned with intense birth pangs. Then, when He ascended to heaven and sent the Holy Spirit, Jesus passed the torch to Him. When the Holy Spirit came on the Day of Pentecost (Acts 2), He took up Jesus' groaning ministry. In other words, the way Jesus travailed on the cross is the way the Holy Spirit continues to travail today.

Why is the Holy Spirit in groaning birth pangs right now? Because things aren't right in the world (see Rom 8). Jesus paid the price for the fullness of the kingdom of God to be established on earth, but what we see today is only a partial manifestation of kingdom fullness. While we're in this partial manifestation, the Holy Spirit continues to travail for the completed work of Calvary to be fully manifest in the earth.

In Romans 8, Paul explained that three things are groaning right now in the throes of distress and intercession. First, all of *creation* is groaning in birth pangs because things aren't right in the world (v 22). Second, *believers* groan within themselves and for the same reason—because things aren't right in our world (v 23). And third, the *Holy Spirit* groans—because things aren't right in this world (v 26).

The Holy Spirit's groans join with ours almost in a symbiotic manner to accelerate the purposes of God in the earth. As He helps us pray, we learn to partner with the Spirit's groans of intercession. This travailing partnership with the Holy Spirit makes our prayers much more effective (Rom 8:26–27).

Paul was describing a kind of prayer that happens only when we groan together in partnership with the Holy Spirit (Rom 8:26). If I'm reading Romans 8 correctly, the Holy Spirit doesn't groan independently of us. In other words, He's not somewhere over on the side, groaning to the Father on our behalf. Rather, He's waiting for us to initiate and engage His groaning ministry with our own spirit. He starts only when we start. When we go to our spirit and engage with His Spirit, His groans of intercession are released through us. If we don't engage with Him in this way, His intercessions for us are paused. The only time He intercedes for us in childbirth is when we engage with Him from our spirit in groaning prayer.

Why is this important? Because when our spirit connects with His Spirit, and when we become the conduit to release His intercessory groanings, we get the Spirit praying God-sized prayers for us according to the will of God (Rom 8:27). The potential of this kind of praying is limitless because of the Holy Spirit's unrestricted power to change anything and everything.

Practice this kind of praying. Go to your spirit and learn how to release the groans of the Holy Spirit. Ask Jesus to teach you how to groan in intercession, together with the Holy Spirit, until kingdom realities are birthed in our generation.

PREGNANT WITH PROMISE

You're pregnant with Promise. That's why you're so hungry right now. That's why you can't seem to get enough of God's word right now. You're eating double. When you're growing a Promise in your spirit, it's *never* enough of His word, promises, assurances, and truth.

When you get a Promise from God, you don't kick back and chill as though it's all in the pocket. You don't *relax* your word intake; you *ramp up* your word intake. Why? Because you've got Promise in your spirit, and now you need to grow that baby.

When some people get a Promise from God, they neglect and starve it out. When we don't feed Promise, instead of birthing God's purpose we just break wind. Isaiah wrote about this:

> We have been with child, we have been in pain; we have, as it were, brought forth wind; we have not accomplished any deliverance in the earth, nor have the inhabitants of the world fallen (Isa 26:18).

Isaiah was writing about people who get pregnant with purpose but end up just passing gas because they didn't grow their Promise in their spirit. Let's heed his caution. What a tragedy it would be to walk for months and years toward God's purpose, but then instead of birthing His purpose through our devotion to Him, we just pass gas.

When we get a Promise from God, therefore, we're not going to kick back and chill; we're going to step up and run the race set before us, looking to Jesus' example, until we see the fulfillment of His purpose in our lives.

According to Isaiah 26:18, God intends that we carry something real in our spirits, grow it, bring it to full term, push, and birth something substantial in the earth. If we do, we can accomplish *deliverance in the earth*—that is, others will be delivered from bondage through the authority of our message and faith. And with the phrase, *the inhabitants of the world fallen*, we're meant to understand that unbelievers will fall before the Lord in repentance and faith because of the race we've run.

Let's birth this thing! So much is at stake! Feed your Promise, grow it, bring it to full term, push, and birth God's purpose for your family.

Promise requires a high-calorie intake in the word of God in order to develop and grow. It needs lots of faith food. When you abide in the words of Christ, you're growing that baby!

When you have a Promise from God, you don't *relax* your prayer life, you *ramp up* your prayer life. You're like, "Lord, now that You've given me this wonderful Promise, You're never going to hear the end of it! I'm going to badger heaven nonstop, day and night, until You fulfill this Promise in my life" (see Luke 18:7).

It's time to intensify your prayer life. Turn the fire up seven times hotter, partner with the Holy Spirit's groaning, and birth the thing.

Somebody might say, "This fiery trial is *killing* me!" But God says, "I don't see a tomb. I see a womb."

IT'S NOT A TOMB . . .

JESUS SHOWED US, through His example on the cross, that what we view as a tomb in our lives is often intended by God to be a womb that births eternal life. Once you awaken to the womb principle of John 16:21, you start to see it all over the Bible.

In the pages that follow, we're going to explore the womb metaphor as seen in several Bible stories, and then draw personal encouragement for our own lives. You'll relate personally to some of these heroes if you've ever been enslaved (Jacob), banished (John), widowed (Anna), silenced (Zacharias), imprisoned (Joseph), bereaved (Naomi), targeted (Mordecai), detoured (Caleb), or crushed (Job).

Let's start with Jacob and the Egyptian slavery. Your faith will grow, while reading the next chapter, when you realize that Israel's slavery was a womb. And then stay engaged for all eleven chapters. With each chapter, you'll get to know a Bible hero better and your heart will soar with growing confidence that Christ is redeeming your circumstances as a womb to birth kingdom purpose.

. . . IT'S A WOMB

FOR SMALL GROUPS

1. Talk about the John 16:21 metaphor of the cross as childbirth. How does that metaphor speak to you personally?

2. "Every advance in the kingdom is preceded by a setback." In what ways have you experienced that?

3. "The nails were His friends." What does that statement mean to you? If there are any mothers in the group, did you experience your contractions as friends to help you push?

4. Have you had an experience in which pain became your friend? Share your story.

5. Do you agree with the author, that the seat of the human spirit is in the upper belly area? Is it helpful for you to connect there with the Holy Spirit?

6. Do you have a promise from God that you're growing in your spirit right now?

PRAY TOGETHER

Is there something painful in your life that you're harnessing like birth pangs, so that something redemptive can be birthed from it? Allow the group to pray with you.

2

ENSLAVED

Jacob's family was enslaved in the nation of Egypt for four hundred and thirty years. That's the testimony of this verse:

> Now the sojourn of the children of Israel who lived in Egypt was four hundred and thirty years. And it came to pass at the end of the four hundred and thirty years—on that very same day—it came to pass that all the armies of the LORD went out from the land of Egypt (Exod 12:40-41).

For four hundred and thirty years, Egypt was a womb for the people of Israel, and I want to show it to you.[1]

GOD SENT A FAMINE

When Jacob's family was only seventy in number, they were living in Canaan and seemed happy enough to remain there. After all,

---

1. Because of Gal 3:17, some scholars estimate that the people of Israel lived inside Egypt for closer to two hundred and twenty years. In Gal 3:17, Paul indicated that the four hundred and thirty years dated back to the time of Abraham, not to the time when Israel entered Egypt. Whether Israel was inside Egypt for four hundred and thirty years or for more like two hundred and twenty years, the point of this chapter applies either way.

it was their Promised Land. But God had other plans for the family, and He began to make their living conditions in Canaan very uncomfortable. How? By sending a famine.

God's history with famines in Scripture is quite intriguing. He's the God of the Famine. He's really good at doing famines. He knows how to use them strategically in our lives to starve us out of where we are, and make us willing to sojourn so that we'll move toward His intended purpose. God needed to move Jacob's family to Egypt, and He used a famine to dislodge them from their settlement.

The famine was devastating for Jacob's family. They lost their crops, they struggled to keep their flocks and herds alive, and they ran out of trading goods they could barter in order to survive. Reduced to poverty and gnawing hunger, Jacob became so desperate that he finally allowed his son Benjamin to go to Egypt with his ten brothers. When the eleven traveled to Egypt to buy more food, the rest of the story was able to unfold.

By the way, God still uses famines in our lives in similar ways. He'll starve us out and reduce us to holy desperation so that we're willing to do whatever it takes to keep moving forward with Him.

Because we have the book of Genesis, we know that the years Jacob's family stayed in Egypt were extremely difficult. They were subjected to slavery, hard labor, and abusive oppression. Furthermore, their male babies were being slaughtered at birth by the Egyptians. Everything about their living conditions under Pharaoh spelled T-O-M-B. Egypt was *killing* them. Why would God do this to Jacob's family?

Let me suggest an answer.

WAR WAS A KILLER

In ancient times, the foremost killer of human populations was war. One of the primary roles of kings in those days was to enrich their nation, and one of the fastest ways to do that was to invade nearby nations, overcome them, and plunder their goods. Everybody was after everybody else's plunder. Egos and ambitions abounded. This Type-A king would take on that Type-A king, looking for a quick way to enrich his constituency. Consequently, large swaths of the population would be repeatedly taken out because of war.

If God had left Jacob and his little family nestled inside Canaan, over the decades they would have been repetitively bombarded with warfare from all sides. Thus, the population base of the family would have been continually eroded, and Jacob's family would have struggled to ever become the size of a nation. But they needed to become a populous nation so they could conquer and possess their Promised Land.

God's solution? He decided to place Jacob's family in a protective womb where they could grow and become a nation. That protective womb was the land of Egypt.

Jacob didn't know it, but God was basically saying, "Let Me do you a favor, Jacob. I'm going to protect your family by placing them behind the front lines of the best equipped military on the planet—the armies of Egypt."

For over two hundred years, Jacob's family was protected by the world's strongest military. For over two hundred years, the armies of Egypt absorbed all the hits from neighboring enemies. For over two hundred years, Jacob's family didn't suffer a single casualty to war. They just kept growing.

ISRAEL GREW INSIDE EGYPT

Oh, the wisdom of God! For over two hundred years, Egypt's population was kept at bay because of border battles, and Jacob's family just kept increasing. Israel multiplied while Egypt picked up the tab.

Israel grew so large—so fast—that by the time they came out of Egypt, Jacob's little family of seventy had grown in size to rival the population of Egypt itself. Exodus 12:37–38 tells us that six hundred thousand men came out of Egypt, plus women and children, plus a mixed multitude of people from other ethnicities. Some scholars estimate, therefore, that Israel's total population at the exodus from Egypt was around three million strong.

When Israel came out of the womb of Egypt, they emerged a *nation*. Isaiah asked, "Shall a nation be born at once?" (Isa 66:8). In Israel's case, the answer would be *yes*. The baby came out a nation.

Overwhelming contractions had birthed an enormous baby.

Israel had grown so large during their centuries of captivity in Egypt that, by the time they came out, they were large enough to enter their Promised Land, take their Promised Land, inhabit their Promised Land, and hold onto their Promised Land.

The book of Psalms says it this way: "Jacob dwelt in the land of Ham. He increased His people greatly, and made them stronger than their enemies" (Ps 105:23–24). We don't know whether Israel was stronger than Egypt in *population* at the exodus, but we do know they were stronger in *warfare*. By the end of the Red Sea crossing, Israel was free from their slavery, and Egypt's armies were drowned in the waters.

GOD IS GROWING YOU

Here's the principle of our story: God puts you into captivity to enlarge you.

Captivity is a womb. But when you first land there, it doesn't feel like a womb. Rather than enlarging you, captivity feels like it's constricting, confining, and inhibiting. But think about it—that's exactly what it feels like inside a womb. You can't get much more confined than a womb. Talk about cramped quarters!

In a womb, you have loss of movement, loss of options, loss of self-determination, loss of identity, loss of control. You can't be innovative or creative. You can't knock stuff off your bucket list. You can't chase after any dreams or aspirations. You lose your capacity for vision-casting. About the only thing you can do in a womb is hang in there and *grow*.

Why are you in this womb? Because God is growing you.

If you're in a place of restriction or confinement, use the time to get large. It's time to go deep in God. Grow in intimacy with Jesus; grow in understanding in the word; grow in the knowledge of Christ; grow in righteousness; grow in holiness; grow in fasting and prayer; grow in good works; grow in humility; grow in the fear of the Lord; grow in love; grow in grace; grow in faith. It's time to get large.

Never waste a good prison sentence.

Turn your prison into an incubator. Is it possible that you could so grow in this place of confinement that the prison can no longer hold you?

Is it possible that you could so grow in your captivity that, by the time you come out, you'll be large enough in the grace of God to *enter* your promises, *take* your promises, *inhabit* your promises, and *hold onto* your promises?

To God, the enslavement in Egypt was a womb that enabled Jacob's family to become a nation. But at the time, Israel couldn't see it. All they could see was the oppression they were suffering. I can imagine them saying to one another, "They're drowning our babies at birth. They're crushing us with torture and grueling slave labor. This place is *killing* us. It's our cemetery!"

But God was going, *I don't see a tomb, I see a womb.*

FOR SMALL GROUPS

1. When you view Egypt as a womb for Israel, what implications do you see in that picture?
2. What connection do you see between the intensity of the sufferings of Israel in Egypt and the birthing of a nation?
3. God used a famine to get Israel to move down to Egypt. Are there any other famines in Scripture that God used in a redemptive way in the lives of people? How does the famine metaphor apply to your life personally? Would you want to tell us about a famine you experienced?
4. "Israel multiplied while Egypt picked up the tab." Got anything you want to say about that?
5. "God puts you into captivity to enlarge you." Can you think of any Bible stories that illustrate that truth? Got a story from your family or friends that illustrates it?
6. "Use the time to get large." What can we do, in practical ways, to fulfill that imperative?

PRAY TOGETHER

Is anyone in our group in a famine right now? What kind of famine is it? Let's pray for those individuals, and ask God to enlarge them in this season.

3

BANISHED

When he was in his nineties, John was banished by Caesar to the prison island of Patmos. According to the writings of Tertullian, they had boiled John in oil in an attempt to kill him, yet he survived. It's possible that Emperor Titus Flavius Domitianus didn't know what else to do with the old man, so he shipped him off to Patmos. The idea was probably to place him in such a remote location that he would no longer be able to spread his message and influence people for the gospel of Christ.

Titus had no idea that Patmos would be John's womb.

Patmos was walled in only by the ocean. There were no buildings to this prison, no cafeteria, no dormitory. It was just a forested rock in the middle of the Mediterranean Sea.

Banish the old man to Patmos, I imagine Caesar thinking. *Let it be his tomb.*

As the boat pulled into Patmos, I wonder if John looked at his new home and thought to himself, *Well, I guess I'm going to die here.* But God was like, *I don't see a tomb.*

Here's how God thinks:

"For My thoughts are not your thoughts, nor are your ways My ways," says the LORD. "For as the heavens are higher than the earth, so are My ways higher than your ways, and My thoughts than your thoughts" (Isa 55:8–9).

That's God's way of saying, "I agree with you about mostly nothing." He doesn't agree with our perspective on our trials because He sees them from a much different vantage. We're often stuck on an earthly outlook, but He sees our trials from a heavenly, eternal perspective.

The walk of faith is the quest to renew our minds in His word until we come to view our circumstances the same way He does.

I think God was engineering John's transfer to Patmos, and He found in Caesar a willing accomplice. I imagine God thinking, *Thanks for the assistance, Caesar. I've been looking for the best way to get John's attention. He's been really distracted and busy recently, going here and there, serving all the churches and laboring diligently for the kingdom. But I've been wanting to get him in a quiet place, without distractions, so I can show him some stuff. Thanks, Caesar, Patmos is perfect. I appreciate the help.*

IN THE SPIRIT

John wrote from his island shanty, "I was in the Spirit on the Lord's Day" (Rev 1:10). I reckon John's practice was to get in the Spirit *every* day, but on this particular occasion it happened to be the Lord's Day.

What was the Lord's Day? Resurrection Day. Jesus rose from the dead on the first day of the week—on Sunday. Most Christian churches convene their weekly gatherings on Sundays in celebration of the Lord's resurrection. For us, *every* Sunday is Easter.

Since it was Resurrection Day, I think it's safe to assume that, in his meditations that day, John was contemplating the resurrection. The thoughts of his heart were probably on the risen

Christ, on the power of His resurrection, and on the overflowing life that resides in Christ.

But John wasn't feeling any of it. For starters, he wasn't feeling any resurrection power in his body, being as old as he was. Instead of his body pulsating with resurrection life, it was complaining to him. He had aches and pains from head to foot, such as is common to nonagenarians. And he didn't have any aspirin or Tylenol to mitigate his discomforts.

Furthermore, he probably wasn't sleeping all that well. Living in a makeshift hut he had built for himself, his homemade mattress was flat and uneven. His clothes were dirty and his body odor foul.

What's more, he was probably hungry, and the few kinds of foods available to him were neither savory nor satisfying.

In other words, with regard to his five senses, he had no sense of connection to the power of Christ's resurrection. His body was uncomfortable and his soul lonely for consoling companionship. Yes, Christ was overflowing with resurrection life, but John couldn't feel any of it. Instead of sensations of resurrection in his body, it felt more like he was carrying the sentence of death.

When we consider the burden on John's body and soul while on Patmos, it becomes all the more striking to hear him say, "I was in the Spirit on the Lord's Day" (Rev 1:10). He was worshiping his Lord, even though he had no music to inspire his song. He was loving his Lord, even though it seemed that heaven greeted his prayers with silence. He was meditating on the resurrection power of Christ, even though none of that power seemed to be making its way personally to him. He knew he was blessed with every spiritual blessing (Eph 1:3), but the blessings seemed to be in heavenly places rather than on his island.

Do you feel like there's a disconnect between the power of Christ and your own personal experience? Is there a chasm between the things Christ provided on His cross and the blessings you're actually experiencing? Does it feel like there's a hundred miles between your Promised Land and the territory you're inhabiting? If so, then you can probably identify with how John must have felt on Patmos. His theology was excellent, but Christianity wasn't working very well for him at the moment.

But that didn't stop him from loving his Lord. He still got in the Spirit on the Lord's Day.

And heaven noticed.

UNSTOPPABLE

Caesar banished John to silence him, but ended up handing him a megaphone. When John decided to do his prison from his spirit, Patmos became the platform for a trumpet blast heard round the world.

What can you do to a man who decides to do his prison from his spirit?

John didn't go to his emotions (intestines), and he didn't go to his convictions (heart), but he went to his spirit (upper gut vicinity).

You can't stop this. There is no stopping the man who does his prison from his spirit.

Caesar could banish John from civilization, but he couldn't banish him from the throne zone.

When John got in the Spirit on the Lord's Day, he was joining himself to the Spirit of God. This is what Paul was referring to when he wrote, "But he who is joined to the Lord is one spirit with Him" (1 Cor 6:17). In the Spirit, John was joined in intimacy and faith to Christ.

In the Spirit. This is the realm of unlimited Holy Spirit, unstoppable Holy Spirit, unrestricted Holy Spirit, unrestrained Holy Spirit, unhindered Holy Spirit, unconfined Holy Spirit, uncontainable Holy Spirit.

You can be chained, but the Spirit of God can't be. There are no limits to the Holy Spirit of God. In the Spirit realm, there are no time limitations, no distance limitations, no spatial limitations, no resource limitations, no financial limitations, no option limitations, no power limitations. When you're in the Spirit, you can go anywhere and do anything that God wants you to do.

When John got in the Spirit, Jesus paid him a personal visit.

Caesar might be able to keep John from getting out of his prison, but he couldn't stop Jesus from getting in. The Man whose feet are like fine brass walks anywhere He wants (Rev 1:15). He walks on whitecapped waves, on fiery stones, on swirling clouds, in blazing furnaces, through gale-force winds, and through cement walls. He's always walking into prison cells, and nobody can stop Him!

When Jesus joined John in his cell, that's when it all began to tumble. Jesus in heaven was remote and distant, as it were; John by himself was isolated and powerless. But when Jesus and John paired up on a remote island, they changed history together.

When Jesus teams up with you, the two of you together are unstoppable.

PATMOS WAS A WOMB

Caesar thought that Patmos would be John's tomb, but when John got in the Spirit on the Lord's Day, the tomb turned into a womb.

In what way did Patmos become a womb? In the sense that the prison island of Patmos gave birth to the book of Revelation. That's where John wrote his Revelation of Christ.

The book of Revelation! It's arguably the most dangerous book in your Bible. That book has rumbled through the centuries of human history, and it's still rumbling in the earth today. Just by birthing the book of Revelation on Patmos, John disrupted and shifted world history.

Caesar thought John was dangerous because he had influence with people. What he didn't understand was that John was dangerous because he had influence with God. Wisdom pursues influence with God, not people. Why would you seek the honor of people when you can seek the honor that comes from the only God (John 5:44)?

The most powerful man on the planet (Caesar) tried to close a door on John, but the most powerful Man in the universe pulled it wide open. When He opens a door, there's not a creature in heaven or hell who can close it (Rev 3:7).

Caesar thought he was taking John out of the game, but Jesus used John's banishment to produce the greatest impact of his entire life. To use baseball language, Patmos became John's grand slam.

When he first arrived at Patmos, John probably thought, *I suppose this island is going to be my tomb.*

But God saw it differently. *It's not a tomb, it's a womb.*

Get in the Spirit and step into the expansive realms of the unfettered Spirit of God. Give Him room to turn your tomb into a womb.

FOR SMALL GROUPS

1. Talk about Isaiah 55:8–9. What are some things in our nation that our generation views very differently from God?
2. God put John on Patmos to get him still. Has the Lord ever put you in a solitary place so He could speak to you more effectively?
3. Talk about the Lord's Day. Has the Lord given you any convictions about the Lord's Day that you honor? On Sundays, do you focus specifically on the resurrection?
4. What's your favorite verse in Revelation 1? Why?
5. "Wisdom pursues influence with God, not people." Explain why you agree or disagree with that statement.
6. Psalm 110:3 called Jesus' secret place relationship with His Father "the womb of the morning." It seems He got in the Spirit just like John did. In what way is your secret place a womb of the morning?

PRAY TOGETHER

Each one of us wants to grow in our ability to get in the Spirit like John did. What are you asking God to give you in this realm? How can we agree together with you in prayer for this?

4

WIDOWED

A widow named Anna pulled Baby Jesus out of a crowd in the temple, and prophesied to those present that He would bring redemption to Jerusalem. The biblical record of her life is brief, so here it is in full:

> Now there was one, Anna, a prophetess, the daughter of Phanuel, of the tribe of Asher. She was of a great age, and had lived with a husband seven years from her virginity; and this woman was a widow of about eighty-four years, who did not depart from the temple, but served God with fastings and prayers night and day. And coming in that instant she gave thanks to the Lord, and spoke of Him to all those who looked for redemption in Jerusalem (Luke 2:36–38).

Anna probably married in her teens, lost her husband in her twenties, and then was eighty-four years old when Jesus was born. Full of the Holy Spirit, she identified Baby Jesus as the Messiah and gave thanks for His coming.

Anna's is a redemption story, and I want to show it to you.

REDEMPTION STORIES

There are several really compelling redemption stories in Scripture. If you accept my definition of a redemption story, then the list of people in Scripture who experienced such a story is not that long. Here's my list: Job, Abraham, Jacob, Joseph, Naomi, Hannah, David, Mordecai, Anna, Elizabeth, and Jesus. Some would argue for others to be added to the list, such as Caleb, Jeremiah, Paul, and John. However you compile the list, Anna's redemption story is one of comparatively few in Scripture.

How might we define a redemption story? For me, a good redemption story has seven elements:

1. The story usually starts with initial serenity and happiness.
2. In a dramatic turn, the protagonist suffers deep, agonizing losses. The story is powerful and compelling because the losses are so very *real*.
3. To all appearances, there is virtually no hope of recovery from the losses.
4. After years of grief, the protagonist experiences a startling reversal in which there is remarkable restoration, vindication, and honor.
5. Sometimes, the protagonist carries permanent scars from the ordeal that testify to the intensity of the hardships endured.
6. Although some losses are never recovered, greater advantages are enjoyed in the end than if the tragedy had never happened.
7. When people see the salvation of God in the protagonist's life, they glorify Him for His goodness and marvel at His mercy.

As we review Anna's story, I think you'll see how most of the above seven elements were present in her narrative.

Anna's story started in comparative serenity. She had hopes for a happy marriage and a rewarding family, but the serenity lasted for only seven years.

The agonizing loss in Anna's life was the death of her husband, who died seven years into their marriage. She was left without husband and children in an era when widowhood was utterly devastating. Her husband meant everything to her—her provider, her protector, her hope for a family, and her lifelong companion. With his death, she faced a lonely, childless, and indigent existence. Bright and hopeful dreams were replaced with despondency and daily scraping to survive.

I wonder how long she sat and stared at her husband's tomb. Even when she wasn't facing it, she lived under its shadow. It embodied her grief and the death of all her aspirations. That tomb dominated her horizon. It loomed over her like a dark cloud that forecasted a lifetime of misery and barrenness.

All she could see was a tomb.

HER CALL TO PRAYER

When God took her husband's life, Anna had a choice. She could become embittered and disengaged from the Lord, or she could set her heart to pursue Him more desperately than ever before. She made the right choice.

I imagine her praying, "Lord, I don't get it. I've been faithful to You, loving You, serving You, walking in obedience to Your law, and You've taken from me all hope of a fulfilling life. Serving You doesn't work."

And I imagine the Lord answering, "Deeper, Anna. Go deeper."

"Lord, I've only asked one thing of You, because there's really only one thing that I've ever wanted in life. All I've ever wanted is to be a faithful wife and mother. And now You've taken from me the only thing I've ever asked of You. Who are You, anyway?"

"Deeper. Go deeper, Anna."

At some point in her grief, Anna accepted the invitation and decided to pursue God in a deeper way.

"I believe You're a good God, but I can't see any of Your goodness in my life right now. Nevertheless, I'm going to come after You until I see it.

"I believe You're a merciful God, and even though I can't see any of Your mercy in my life right now, I'm going to come after You until I see it.

"I worship You, Lord, because I believe You're a faithful God. I can't see any of Your faithfulness in my life right now, but I'm going to come after You until I do."

Lifting a sail, she harnessed the blustery gusts of her sorrow and depression, and used the power of those stormy winds to press into the heart of God.

It's not the storms that change us, but the pursuit of God in the storms that changes us.

As she pursued the Lord in prayer, I believe one day she heard the Voice. "Seek Me in the temple. Do it day and night."

She was like, "Okay."

"With fasting and prayer," the Voice added.

"Fasting? Ugh. I hate fasting. Um…This one's tough, but…okay!"

And Anna decided to turn the fire up seven times hotter. She devoted herself, night and day, to fasting and prayer in the temple.

SUFFERING REPROACH

I can imagine a visitor looking at Anna huddled in a corner of the temple and asking a bystander, "Who's that lady in the corner?"

"You don't know who that is? Oh, you must be new to town," the bystander said. "That's Anna."

"What's her deal? I mean, she doesn't do anything all day except kneel in the corner and occasionally wipe her eyes. What's her story?"

"It's a very sad story. Unfortunately, she lost her husband."

"Wow, that's tough, I'm so sorry to hear that! When did it happen?"

"Well, that's the sad part. It happened *years* ago, and she's never recovered. It's so heartbreaking to watch. It seems that some people don't know how to handle grief. It's just a tragic waste of a life."

And *nobody* understood Anna. Nobody knew what was going on inside her, but she had a fire in her belly, and the Spirit of God was resting upon her.

She was developing a responsiveness to the Holy Spirit that would recognize the Messiah when He came. When the Messiah was finally born, the people that should have discerned His coming (the priests and spiritual leaders) didn't, and a childless widow curled up on the floor of the temple did.

MESSIAH

As the months turned into years and the years into decades, I think Anna heard the Voice again, whispering, "Messiah."

"Messiah??" I hear her gasping. "Is *that* what this is about?"

When she got that word, everything changed. Something took hold of her spirit, as though she were in the birth pangs of labor. Curled into a fetal position, she travailed in intercession for the coming of the King. Holy contractions took hold of her spirit, and she began to groan.

I can imagine her thinking, *I've never given birth to a baby before—that privilege was stripped from me—so I'm not exactly sure what childbirth feels like. But this feels like childbirth. It feels like I'm giving birth to something.*

Yes, Anna, you are! *You're giving birth to the Messiah through your intercessory ministry.*

God needed an intercessor to accomplish in the Spirit what Mary would accomplish in the natural, in order to bring to birth His redemptive purposes. Anna's decades of intercessory ministry were vindicated when she held in her arms the answer to her prayers.

JOHN THE BAPTIST

In the days of Anna, Zacharias the priest had a tour of duty in Jerusalem. On a certain day, he was selected by lot to offer up incense in the inner court of the temple. As he performed that service, the angel Gabriel appeared and told Zacharias that his wife, Elizabeth, was going to give birth to a miracle baby—whom we know as John the Baptist. When Zacharias received this news from the angel, Anna was just a few feet away in the outer court of the temple, praying. It seems, therefore, that through her intercessory ministry Anna birthed not only the Messiah but also His forerunner, John the Baptist.

Her travailing prayers made a way, in the Spirit, for Gabriel to come to both Zacharias and Mary with his glorious announcements of supernatural pregnancies—those of John the Baptist and Jesus. Her intercession mobilized angels.

After Anna held Jesus in her arms, she "spoke of Him to all those who looked for redemption in Jerusalem" (Luke 2:38). There were people in Jerusalem looking for redemption, and when Anna declared the Lord's redemption, their hearts filled with hope and expectation. The same kinds of people are also with us here and now in this generation. Of all the believers in the body of Christ, there are some who are constantly on the lookout for redemption and divine intervention—that is, for the invasion of Glory into the human sphere. Never satisfied with status quo, they're longing for heaven to break in and disrupt the natural order of things. They want God to do something God-sized in this generation. They're the ones who will rejoice with you when God turns your tomb into a womb.

A MOTHER IN ISRAEL

When Anna held Baby Jesus in her arms, she held the fruit of decades of laborious intercession.

Someone might say that Anna died childless, but I see her as a mother in Israel who gave birth to the Messiah through her intercession. What a mighty Baby to birth! Now, *millions* of believers look back on Anna as a spiritual mother because she birthed our Redeemer through her faithful ministry to the Lord.

Anna's story was a redemption story. She thought she would die childless, when in fact she died with a quiver of millions. When she birthed the Messiah through her labors, she ended up giving birth to much more than simply a little family in her community; she gave birth, in one sense, to millions of believers across all the nations and throughout all the halls of church history. *A mother to millions!* The redemption element in her story is really stunning. She came into a motherhood that is so much greater than if her husband had not died prematurely.

Living in the shadow of a tomb, her obedience became a womb.

FOR SMALL GROUPS

1. Read Luke 2:36–38 together. How does Anna's example speak to your life? How does her obedience inspire you?
2. Talk about the author's idea of "Redemption Stories," and look at the seven elements he listed. Is there anything you'd want to delete or add to the list?
3. What's your favorite redemption story in the Bible? Why?
4. Have you experienced a tragedy that caused you to go deeper in prayer? What did you learn about prayer in that season?
5. Do you agree with the author that, through her intercessory ministry, Anna birthed the ministries of John the Baptist and Jesus?
6. Jesus' metaphor of childbirth in John 16:21 is brilliant as it relates to our fiery trials because it does two things: a) It dignifies our sufferings, and b) it strengthens our hope that God is birthing something significant through them. Are you comforted by the way Jesus dignifies your sufferings through this metaphor?

PRAY TOGETHER

Let's ask the Lord to help us go deeper in prayer, especially in our times of struggle. Is there a specific way you want the Lord to help you go deeper in prayer? We'll agree with your prayer.

5

SILENCED

Zacharias and Elizabeth were an elderly couple who were contemporaries of Anna and who had a redemption story of their own.

Scripture testified to this couple's godliness:

> And they were both righteous before God, walking in all the commandments and ordinances of the Lord blameless. But they had no child, because Elizabeth was barren, and they were both well advanced in years (Luke 1:6–7).

Zacharias and Elizabeth were childless in a society where heritage was entirely wrapped up in one's posterity. But they had no son to carry the family name, no one to perpetuate the legacy of generations, no children to bequeath an inheritance. It appeared that their family heritage would die with them. To Elizabeth, her barrenness was like a tomb.

REPROACH

Elizabeth must have felt incredible reproach for her barrenness. After all, Psalm 127:3 said, "The fruit of the womb is a reward."

Since children were a reward from God, some folks took that to mean that barrenness was punishment from God. Some probably viewed Elizabeth as cursed by God for something she or her ancestors had done (see John 9:2).

We can only imagine the kind of grief and reproach that Elizabeth endured through the decades. She probably wondered, *Have I sinned? What did I do wrong?* We don't know how many tears she shed, how many prayers she offered, or how many times she pled with God to show her what was hindering the blessing. How often did she throw herself upon her bed, bury her face in the pillow, and wail in gut-wrenching agony? We just don't know.

Have you ever talked to a wife who has tried unsuccessfully for years to get pregnant or bring a baby to full term? For some, the anguish is overwhelming. For those of us who haven't experienced barrenness, how could we possibly understand the depth of Elizabeth's grief and pain?

Elizabeth was not only barren, but she was also "well advanced in years." Now that she had moved past her childbearing years, in one sense she was doubly barren. Every remote hope of ever possibly having a baby had died.

Elizabeth was probably plagued by at least three voices: Reproach from people, accusation from the devil, and her own self-questioning.

BLAMELESS

But in the midst of all the reproachful voices, she devoted herself to righteous living. Both she and Zacharias continued to walk blamelessly before their God.

Not everyone, in the face of such heartache, maintains a blameless walk. Why not? Because it's very tempting, in the face of grueling disappointment, to indulge the flesh. The tempter comes to us when we're weak and discouraged, and says things like, "You deserve this. It doesn't really matter if it's an illegal pleasure, God understands. Go ahead. Enjoy."

But Zacharias and Elizabeth refused to allow disappointment to turn them from their devotion to holiness. They had come to know too much of the Lord's goodness to sacrifice their inheritance on the altar of carnal passion. They were committed to loving and serving God faithfully, even if He never answered their prayer.

Consequently, God had mercy on Elizabeth and gave her a baby. But not just any baby—Elizabeth got John the Baptist! She went down in history as the barren woman who gave birth to a prophet, yea, more than a prophet. Just as Elijah made room for Elisha, John prepared a way for Jesus. She gave birth to Jesus' forerunner.

Her tomb became a womb.

That's Elizabeth.

Now let's talk about her husband Zacharias. Elizabeth's tomb was barrenness, but Zacharias faced a tomb related to his voice.

ZACHARIAS

Zacharias was a priest who traveled occasionally to Jerusalem to perform his appointed temple duties. On one such trip, he was burning incense in the temple when he was visited suddenly by the angel Gabriel (see Luke 1:6–23).

The first thing Gabriel said was, "Do not be afraid, Zacharias, for your prayer is heard; and your wife Elizabeth will bear you a son, and you shall call his name John" (Luke 1:13). Gabriel said *your prayer*, not *your prayers*. It seems that Zacharias had only one prayer. When you're barren, you have just one prayer: "Give me a child."

Zacharias had what Lou Engle calls *a life-dominating prayer*. A tomb has a way of giving you a life-dominating prayer. When facing a tomb, your petitions focus on the one thing that preoccupies your mind and dominates your desires.

When you have a life-dominating prayer, it'll come to mind repeatedly throughout your day. All the powers of your soul bear down on that one desire as you cry to God for heaven's intervention. When your soul reaches for God with that kind of focused desperation, you're praying the kind of prayer that heaven hears.

Chances are that Zacharias had stopped asking for a baby. I mean, Elizabeth was now past her childbearing years, and all hopes for a pregnancy were dead and buried. But God had not forgotten the prayers Zacharias had offered for so many decades. Those prayers lingered in His presence like incense hanging in the air (see Ps 141:2). God had said, "When I choose the proper time, I will judge uprightly," and now the proper time had come (Ps 75:2). Zacharias would have a son and would call his name John.

Gabriel then went on to describe John's calling and ministry (Luke 1:14–17). Zacharias responded with a question, "How shall I know this? For I am an old man, and my wife is well advanced in years" (Luke 1:18). There's nothing wrong with asking God questions, but the Lord perceived that this question proceeded from a hardened, unbelieving heart.

God chose to discipline Zacharias, therefore, and made him mute. He was *silenced* by God. But Gabriel's announcement of the affliction also came with a promise: "You will be mute and not able to speak until the day these things take place" (Luke 1:20). The duration of the affliction would be unknown to Zacharias, but he was assured the silencing was temporary. At the right time, his voice would open again.

Zacharias had prayed for a baby for so long that, after years of unanswered prayers, he had become heartsick and unbelieving. When the mighty angel Gabriel finally came with the answer, Zacharias's heart was so crusty and hardened by disappointment that he simply couldn't respond in faith—not even to a visitation by a powerful angel. He had too many years behind him of dashed dreams and unfulfilled hopes. Life had been too hard. Forty-plus years of deferred hope had made this heartsick man incapable of responding in faith to Gabriel's glorious announcement.

But Zacharias's unbelief was a problem. Why? Because God needed John the Baptist, and to get him, he needed John to be raised by a father who was living in a spirit of faith.

God had to change Zacharias, and fast! But how? God decided to use His accelerated program—prison. God put him in a prison of physical affliction (muteness is a prison) so that he would be transformed into the spiritual father that John the Baptist needed.

Some people view Zacharias's muteness as God punishing him for his unbelief, as though God were saying, "You didn't believe Me, Zacharias, so I'm slapping you with a fine. Your punishment will be the frustration of not being able to talk until your son is born. I'm going to teach you how displeasing your unbelief is to Me."

But I don't view his muteness as punishment. Rather, I see it as the vehicle God used to revolutionize him rapidly and make him a fitting spiritual father for John the Baptist. It wasn't punishment, it was promotion.

I imagine God thinking something like, *Zacharias, we've got to do some fast work here. John the Baptist needs a prophetic father, and we've only got ten months to make you into that man. In the same way that Joseph's dungeon accelerated his growth curve, this affliction will force you to find a new walk with Me. The intensity of the trial will cause you to press into Me like never before. In My mercy, I'm granting you an opportunity for change. So buckle up. You're going to endure a very trying ordeal. I'm making you deaf and mute.*[2]

To Zacharias, being deaf and mute seemed like being in a tomb, and the devil really wanted him to believe he'd be buried

---

1. Luke 1:62 indicates that Zacharias was not only mute, but also deaf, for they made signs to communicate with him.

in that prison. The only thing Zacharias knew to do was run hard after God and study the things Gabriel had revealed about John. He was desperate to understand Gabriel's proclamation, and that desperate pursuit of God changed him profoundly.

When John was finally born, Zacharias wrote on a tablet, *His name is John*. Immediately his tongue was loosed. What would Zacharias say after roughly ten months of silence? The answer is remarkable. Pouring from his lips came a fiery stream of prophetic declarations that glorified God's purposes in John and the coming Messiah. His oracle in Luke 1:67–79 is really worth taking the time to read. Zacharias came out of the trial with a clear prophetic voice regarding his son's destiny. His transformation was staggering.

Considering how elderly he was, clearly we're never too old to change.

Zacharias! Who are you? Where did you come from? You're nothing like the man of ten months ago. What happened to you?

I hear him answering, "Well, I was facing a tomb. It looked like I would be deaf and mute for the rest of my life. In desperation, I devoted myself to fasting, prayer, pressing into God, and devouring His word. What God showed me in that prison changed my life. When He healed me, I couldn't help but prophesy!"

Zacharias had been silenced by God, and the infirmity felt like a tomb. The trial wasn't a tomb, however, to kill him, but a womb to make him a spiritual father. When he was healed, he emerged from the trial a prophetic voice who could raise and rear John the Baptist.

Your fiery trial isn't a tomb, it's a womb.

FOR SMALL GROUPS

1. Have you ever felt judged by other people because of a difficult trial in your life, as though it indicated sin in your life? How did you process the reproach?
2. Have you ever been tempted, when facing a trial, to indulge the flesh? What did the Lord teach you through that?
3. Have you ever been silenced by God? Want to talk about it?
4. Talk about the transformation that happened in Zacharias through the trial of silence. In what ways did God change him? (The story is in Luke 1.)
5. Do you think Zacharias's trial was punishment or promotion?
6. How did God make Zacharias into a spiritual father? Look at Malachi 4:5–6, and how it might apply to Zacharias's story. How does this speak to you personally?

PRAY TOGETHER

Do you have a life-dominating prayer you'd want to tell the group about? What's your strongest prayer request right now? Tell us how we can agree with you in prayer.

6

IMPRISONED

Everybody loves Joseph's story. Why? Not because of his years in the palace, but because of his years in the prison. His prison years were horrible, but those were the years that put power into his story and made his a redemption story.

What can we learn from Joseph's prison? So much more than I could ever fit into this chapter!

To begin with, God got Joseph into prison, and God got him out. The thing that got Joseph in—walking with God—got him out. Therefore, if God designed your prison, He'll also design your release.

Joseph ended up in prison after doing everything right. When we end up in prison, in some cases it's because we did something wrong, but in other cases it's because we did something right.

Because Joseph experienced a prison sentence, he became a compassionate judge over all the land. Prison turns our judgmentalism into compassion.

Joseph became the man he was through the formative forces of rejection, loneliness, and restriction. God still uses those forces today for your character formation.

Had he kept his eyes on what his brothers did to him, he would have remained a prisoner to their rejection. But because he lifted his eyes to what God was doing in his life, he was liberated to participate in God's higher purposes.

Joseph could forgive because he saw God, not his brothers, as the designer of his destiny. When people do wrong by you, if you'll receive it as from the hand of God, you'll be able to forgive those people and keep moving forward in your upward calling.

God placed Joseph in a vacuum of fatherlessness to make him a spiritual father (Gen 45:8). You don't have to have a spiritual father in order to become one. Rather, let God make you into the spiritual father you never had.

If you end up in prison with a Joseph, become his friend because one day he may have the authority to spring you loose.

The longer you keep a Joseph buried in prison, the higher He'll rise.

Everything changed for Joseph when God gave Pharaoh a dream (Gen 41:1). God can completely change your season simply by giving someone else a dream.

There is no prison that's strong enough to keep a God dream incarcerated forever. Promise trumps prison.

Joseph named his sons after his story because they embodied the fruit of his journey. They became principal figures in the story. His redemption story wasn't complete until his posterity carried it. God is at work to do the same for your family.

Joseph's prison speaks to so many things in our lives, but so do other parts of his story. Consider, for example, his stewardship in the palace.

STEWARD PRIVILEGE WISELY

When Pharaoh brought Joseph out of prison and gave him authority over the land of Egypt, Joseph decided in his heart, *Pharaoh, you'll never regret giving me this privilege. I'm not going to use it to undermine you; rather, I'm going to use it to make you the wealthiest man on earth.*

By the time the story was done, Joseph had given Pharaoh all the money, all the livestock, and all the land of Egypt. Joseph used his privilege to enrich the man who gave him privilege.

To all the young people reading this, I have some advice for you. *Decide in your heart that no one will ever regret giving you privilege.* If they hired you, paid your way, opened a door for you, promoted you, gave you a seat at the table, connected you strategically, or in some manner granted you privilege, be sure they never regret it. Use your privilege to preserve the interests of the person who gave you that privilege. If you do, you'll be demonstrating the integrity of a Joseph.

JOSEPH'S REGRET

While in prison, Joseph lived with a huge regret: He regretted telling his dreams to his brothers. He was in an Egyptian prison, ultimately, because he spilled his dreams to his brothers. Follow the chain of events. Telling the dreams made them envious; envy caused them to sell him into slavery; slavery meant he couldn't evade Potiphar's wife, and her lies landed him in prison. He was in prison because of his big fat mouth.

Like anyone with a great regret, Joseph replayed the scenes over and over. *Why did I do that? Why did I say that?* He wanted to hit a delete button and undo the whole thing, but he couldn't. What was done was done.

I imagine him sitting in prison and talking to himself, *I'm a motor mouth. I can't keep my mouth shut. Every time God shows me a secret, I have to blab it to the whole world. What's my problem, anyway? For the rest of my life, I'm going to be a prisoner to a stupid, youthful indiscretion.*

The regret was so strong that he was tempted to despair. The voices in his head probably said things like, *You'll never marry or have kids or be productive in life. You have no advocate to get you out of this prison. You have nobody. You're going to die in this hole.*

Regret wanted to overwhelm him with despair, but Joseph decided to redeem the regret and go the other direction with it. It's one of the greatest secrets of his success: *He turned regret into restraint.* He decided to become a keeper of secrets. He became the most tight-lipped man in Egypt. He went from Mr. Motor Mouth to Mr. Zipper Lips.

Joseph's restraint made the story.

JOSEPH'S RESTRAINT

When Joseph was thirty, Pharaoh released him from prison and made him his right-hand man. In one spectacular day, he went from prison to palace. It was a dizzying promotion.

When you're ballistically successful in life, there's one person you especially want to know about it—your father! Joseph wanted his father to know that he had made something with his life. He had become the second most powerful man on the planet! And Joseph had all kinds of means at his disposal to notify his father. He could have dispatched a courier with a letter; he could have sent a group of ambassadors in pomp and circumstance; he could have deployed the Egyptian army, arrested the entire family, brought them all back to Egypt, and then staged a sensational unveiling. Because of his position of power, he had multiple ways he could have revealed this secret to his father.

But he refused to tell. Joseph was sitting on the biggest secret of his life, and he didn't tell his father for nine years. When he got married, he didn't even invite his papa to the wedding. He just shut his trap and kept watching for his brothers.

He knew his brothers would eventually show up. The famine had hit their region hard, and Joseph knew they'd eventually have to come to Egypt for food. That's why he insisted on personally selling food to all the foreigners who came to buy grain; he was watching for his brothers. He didn't go to them, he waited for them to come to him (Jer 15:19).

After his brothers came to Egypt, Joseph *still* restrained himself. On their first trip for food, he didn't reveal his identity to them. Why not? Perhaps because he had seen eleven *brothers* in his dream. On their first visit, only ten brothers came to Egypt. With faith in the dreams God had given him, Joseph knew their first visit was not yet the fulfillment of his dreams.

On the second visit, when all eleven brothers stood before him, he *still* restrained himself—until he could do so no longer. In an overflow of unrestrained tears, he finally revealed his identity to them (Gen 45:1).

GOD RESTRAINS HIMSELF

Restraint is a godly quality. God is *always* restraining Himself with us. When we exercise restraint, we're being godly.

God withholds nothing from us (Ps 84:11), but He does restrain Himself for strategic purposes. The enemy wants to convince us that God is withholding from us, but the cross clearly shows that God withholds nothing from us. At the cross, God gave us His *everything*. He withholds nothing from us, but He does sometimes restrain Himself for a season so He can give us even more in the end.

Joseph's restraint gave his story its drama and suspense. By keeping his lips zipped, he set up one of the most colorful sagas in the entire Bible. Restraint gave God room to work on Joseph's behalf and write a compelling redemption story.

If you have a great regret—perhaps because of your inexperience or because of a youthful indiscretion—turn your regret into restraint. When you pull back in the area where you were once unrestrained, you give God room to write your story His way.

Joseph regretted his mistake, but God didn't. It gave God the material He needed to craft a nail-biting thriller. He's a great Redeemer, and He knows how to turn our liabilities into assets. He's able to redeem our biggest mistakes and make them the best part of our story.

A TOMB?

When Joseph was sent to prison, he probably wondered if it would be his tomb. After all, he had no advocate to plead his case, nor any family in town to bail him out. And the man who put him in prison had the power to keep him there indefinitely.

Joseph probably agonized in prayer, "God, I'm going to die in this prison!" But God didn't see a tomb.

What was God's purpose in the prison? He wanted Joseph to get in touch with his spirit. Let me explain what I mean.

JOSEPH WAS MULTI-GIFTED

Joseph was exceptionally talented and capable. In my opinion, he was a five-talent guy. When I say that, I'm borrowing from the imagery of Jesus' parable in which He said that some people are given five talents, some are given two, and some get one (Matt 25:15).

God had given Joseph five talents. The guy had it cooking on every burner. He had people skills, communication skills, leadership skills, administrative skills, business skills, accounting skills, an entrepreneurial chip, problem-solving abilities, a quick mind, creative ingenuity, charm and charisma, and on top of it all, a buff body. The guy was a five-talent package, and everything he touched turned to gold.

Furthermore, he was diligent to cultivate and grow his gifts and talents. In the language of Jesus' parable, he was faithful to turn five talents into ten (Matt 25:16).

I imagine God thinking, *Joseph, you're good, but you're not good enough. Your talents will take you a long way, but they won't take you to the places I have ordained for you. Your talents will take you part of the way, but I have a higher calling for you—a calling that's higher than your gifts and abilities. For you to steward your destiny and calling, you're going to have to tap into something greater than your talents. You're going to have to discover a realm that's greater than gifts and talents and natural strength, a realm that is not by might or power but by My Spirit. To find it, you've got to learn to live from your spirit.*

At the time, Joseph was roughly twenty years old. Most twenty-year-olds haven't learned yet to live from their spirit. Most of them live from their talents and strengths. But God needed Joseph to find his spirit—fast—so He put him in His accelerated growth program. Prison.

God can do more in a Joseph in ten years of prison than most people obtain in a lifetime.

The prison's purpose was to train Joseph to live from his spirit.

THE WEAKNESS OF FIVE-TALENT PEOPLE

Here's the downside of five-talent people like Joseph: They tend to rely on their gifts and abilities. When you have five talents, all you need to do is work hard, and everything will come your way. Five-talent leaders really don't need to pray to make their business a success. Five-talent worship leaders don't really need to depend on the Holy Spirit to pull off effective church worship services. Five-talent entrepreneurs don't really need to lean on Jesus to become successful and make a lot of money. Five-talent communicators can sway an audience even if God isn't helping them.

Five-talent people don't always reach for the deeper dimensions of the Holy Spirit because they've learned that their gifts and strengths are enough to obtain their objectives.

That's why I can imagine God saying, *Joseph, I'm going to help you find your spirit. To do that, I'm going to shut your talents down. I'm going to put you in a prison where none of your strengths will get you out. When I shut down your talents, you'll be forced to find your spirit.*

When you're in prison, it doesn't matter how strong your leadership skills, they're not going to get you out of prison. It doesn't matter how smart you are, your brains aren't going to get you out of prison. It doesn't matter how sharp your business skills might be, they're not going to get you out of prison. It doesn't matter how charming and personable you are, your charisma and people skills aren't going to get you out of prison. And it doesn't matter what kind of a hunk you are, your good looks aren't going to get you out of prison.

And Joseph found himself in a prison where every talent he had been faithful to cultivate was rendered *useless*.

"I'm going to die in this prison!"

DEEPER

In his interminably foul prison, Joseph began to reach into the heart of God with the desperation of a dying man.

I can hear Joseph saying, "God, I don't get You! I've been faithful to You, loving You, serving You, and living in Your presence. But serving You doesn't work. All that my faithful service has done is land me in this horrible prison."

And all God said was, "Deeper."

"God, I've held to Your promises. You promised things to my great-grandfather Abraham that I cherish and treasure. But holding to Your promises obviously isn't working in my life."

And God persisted, "Deeper."

"But God, I separated myself from my wayward generation. I even said no to Potiphar's wife. And look where my integrity has gotten me. It's gotten me rotting in a sewer! Clearly, serving You doesn't work."

And God just kept saying, "Deeper. Go deeper, son."

DREAM INTERPRETATION

Desperate to somehow survive his tomb, Joseph began to reach into the depths of the Holy Spirit more fervently than he had in his entire life. He had always been a man of prayer, but this was different. This was the frantic clawing of a man desperate to breathe.

In his pursuit of God's heart, he decided to study his God language. Joseph's God language was dreams. In other words, God spoke to Joseph through dreams. When he was younger, God had given him two divine dreams that were clear and extraordinarily compelling. Now, in his prison, he was desperate to know what those dreams meant. He couldn't reconcile the hope of his dreams with the hopelessness of his prison. The dreams seemed to indicate greatness, but his prison screamed, "You're dead!"

"God, what did those dreams mean?"

As he pressed deeper into the Holy Spirit, Joseph studied dream interpretation. He became a student of his God language, and good thing he did! When the butler and baker came to prison and received divine dreams, Joseph was able to interpret their dreams (see Gen 40). Then, when Pharaoh received a divine dream, he was able to interpret Pharaoh's dream (see Gen 41).

Joseph didn't get out of prison because of his multifaceted gift set; he got out of prison because the Spirit of God was living inside him, giving him illumination and understanding (Gen

41:38–39). In one moment, he went from the prison to the palace—because he had gone deep in God and studied his God language.

WHAT'S YOUR GOD LANGUAGE?

That's a great question to ask. In other words, ask yourself, *How does God talk to me?* Too often we get distracted by how He *doesn't* talk to us. Too often we wonder things like, *Why doesn't God talk to me in the same way He talks to my pastor?* That's the wrong question. Stop looking at how God talks to others, and focus instead on how He talks to you. In other words, stop obsessing about how He *doesn't* talk to you, and look instead at how He *does*.

God will come alongside, match the cadence of your stride, and walk with you in a way that's unique to just the two of you. Become skillful in your cadence with God.

God talks to people in all sorts of ways, based upon their unique personality and personhood. He'll likely talk to you differently from the way He talks to your neighbor. God talks to some people through dreams. With others, He talks to them through nature. With many, He talks to them primarily through Scripture. With some, He talks to them through inner impressions. For others, it happens during quiet listening. A sister told me once that God talks to her through colors.

What's your God language? Identify it, study it, and master it. Mastering your God language just might get you out of prison, too.

Through the confinement of his prison, Joseph found a dimension in God he would have never otherwise discovered. He found a dimension that isn't accessed by natural strengths, gifts, or talents. It's a dimension that is, "'Not by might nor by power, but by My Spirit,' says the LORD of hosts" (Zech 4:6).

Joseph needed that depth in God so that he could lead the nation of Egypt through a blistering famine and earn the relational authority with Pharaoh to establish his family in prosperity in the land of Goshen.

GOD'S ACCELERATED PROGRAM

As stated already, prison is God's accelerated program. God used prison in Joseph's life to accelerate his maturity curve. Scripture says that when he was released at age thirty, he taught his elders wisdom (Ps 105:22) and became a father to Pharaoh (Gen 45:8). In other words, he emerged from prison with a wisdom and maturity beyond his years.

Furthermore, Scripture says that he came out of prison with authority, "To bind his princes at his pleasure" (Ps 105:22). After his release, he possessed the authority to incarcerate others in the prison that once held him. Joseph came out carrying the keys to his prison.

He used that authority, for example, with his own brothers. At one point in the story, he imprisoned his ten brothers together for three days (Gen 42:17). I imagine Joseph thinking, *Here's a little sampler for y'all. I did this prison for ten years—I'll let you guys taste it for three days.*

REACH FOR THE KEYS

I have a personal theory about Joseph, and I call it a theory because I can't support my suggestion with a verse. But when Joseph came out of prison—holding the keys to his prison—I think he went back to that prison. I think he paid a visit to the prisoners he had come to know so well. Why? Because when you make friends in prison, and then manage a jailbreak, you want to bring your friends out with you.

I imagine him saying to one of the prisoners, "You actually deserve to stay in prison because of the crime you committed, but you were my faithful friend for ten years, and you're coming out."

To another prisoner he may have said, "You're going to serve on my cabinet as one of my prime ministers. You're coming out!"

To another I've got him saying, "Uh, you'll be staying in, bro."

My point is that when Joseph was finally released from prison, he came out with authority over his prison.

God wants to redeem your prison years in such a way that, when you come out, you arise with authority over the very prison that once held you.

Did you find yourself in a financial prison? By the time you escape from this prison, you'll have the authority to help others who are trapped in prisons of financial difficulty.

Were you imprisoned to an addiction? By the time you gain victory over this prison, you'll be able to help others who are bound in prisons of addiction.

Did you become trapped in a prison of physical infirmity? By the time you gain the spiritual authority to be freed from this prison, you'll be able to loose others who are also bound in prisons of physical infirmity.

Never relent until you hold in your hand the key to the prison that now binds you.

Maybe you feel a little bit like Joseph must have felt in his prison. You may feel like you're shackled by chains that will never relax their grip. You may even feel like a death sentence has been pronounced over you. But may the promises of God lift your eyes in faith to see your prison as God sees it.

When God looks at your prison, He doesn't see a tomb; He sees a womb.

FOR SMALL GROUPS

1. What's your favorite part of Joseph's story? Why? Tell the group.
2. Do you have a story about regretting giving someone privilege, because of the way they stewarded that privilege?
3. In what ways does God restrain Himself with us? In what ways, therefore, should we exercise restraint toward others?
4. "God can do more in a Joseph in ten years of prison than most people obtain in a lifetime." Do you agree with that statement?
5. What's your God language? What can we do to study our God language?
6. "When Joseph was finally released from prison, he came out with authority over his prison." How does that statement give you hope for your journey?

PRAY TOGETHER

Let's ask the Lord to help us identify our God language, study it, and master it.

7

BEREAVED

For me, the book of Ruth has the wrong title. When you open a book entitled *Ruth*, you're fully expecting to read the story of a woman named Ruth. But even though she's a main character in the plot, it's not really her story. It's Naomi's story. Yes, the heroine is Ruth, but the protagonist is Naomi.

The book of Ruth is Naomi's redemption story. The story started with her losses and ended with her redemption.

AGONIZING LOSSES

Naomi's story started in relative serenity. She lived in Bethlehem with her husband Elimelech and their two sons. A famine hit the land, however, and Naomi's husband was too poor to ride it out. Driven from their homestead, they emigrated to Moab to survive.

While in Moab, Naomi's fortunes grew even darker. Her husband died, and she was left a single mom with two sons. Her sons eventually married two Moabite women, but then in the course of time Naomi's two sons also died. She was left a foreigner in Moab, widowed, and bereft of her two sons. She had lost her homestead, husband, sons, protection, support, and security—she had lost *everything*. When she looked at her future, all she could see was grinding poverty and bitter loneliness.

Naomi didn't have a tomb. She didn't have two tombs. She had *three* tombs to stare at—three tombs that confirmed the hand of the Lord had gone out against her (Ruth 1:13).

When word came that the famine had lifted in Bethlehem, she decided to return home. One of her daughters-in-law, Orpah, opted to stay in Moab and rebuild her life. The other daughter-in-law, Ruth, refused to leave Naomi's side but determined to accompany her on the trip back to Bethlehem.

I suggest you pause here and read the book of Ruth before continuing with this chapter. Why? Because if you'll refresh yourself in that book, you'll be set up to appreciate the way this chapter presents Naomi's redemption story.

NAOMI'S GRIEF

When Naomi and Ruth arrived in Bethlehem, the women of the city excitedly asked, "Is this Naomi?" She answered them,

> Do not call me Naomi; call me Mara, for the Almighty has dealt very bitterly with me. I went out full, and the LORD has brought me home again empty. Why do you call me Naomi, since the LORD has testified against me, and the Almighty has afflicted me? (Ruth 1:20–21).

Naomi means *Pleasant*, and *Mara* means *Bitter*. Naomi said to the women, "Call me Bitter." Why? Because life had turned very bitter for her. She left Bethlehem "full," with a husband and two sons, and returned "empty," with neither husband nor sons. God had taken the lives of all her men. The Lord had given to her, but then had taken away (see Job 1:21). Consequently, her soul had sunk into a deep and bitter depression.

Depression is a common response to grief. Loss produces grief, and when we feel trapped by grief, it often leads to depression. Naomi's soul was cast down because she felt trapped by her losses. In her words, the Almighty had bitterly afflicted her. Naomi said it bluntly the way she saw it because, when you're hurting that much, you're not afraid to say exactly how you feel.

When we're depressed, Satan tries to exploit our emotions to squeeze our souls dry of faith. But depression and faith are not mutually exclusive. Just because you're depressed doesn't mean you have to let go of your faith. Like Naomi, you can fight for your faith even amid agonizing losses. Years of depression can be redeemed to grow faith that's authentic and enduring.

Even though she was bitterly afflicted, Naomi still kept her faith in God. It's one of the more stunning aspects of the story, and it positioned her for mercy.

NAOMI'S FAITH

Naomi's faith made the story.

I see the strength of her faith in three places in the book. The first is found in Ruth's vow of loyalty to Naomi. When Naomi suggested that Ruth stay behind in Moab, Ruth replied with these words:

> Entreat me not to leave you, or to turn back from following after you; for wherever you go, I will go; and wherever you lodge, I will lodge; your people shall be my people, and your God, my God. Where you die, I will die, and there will I be buried (Ruth 1:16–17).

Where did Ruth get this faith in the God of Abraham? Principally from Naomi. Let me explain.

Ruth was a native of Moab and, thus, excluded by nationality from God's promises to Abraham and his descendants. But her marriage to Naomi's son had changed all that, and I'm persuaded Naomi had talked to her about it. Naomi probably said to Ruth, "Do you realize what you've done by marrying my son? By marrying into a Jewish family, you've married into the blessings that God gave to Abraham. You now share in all the marvelous blessings and promises that God has given to Abraham's posterity, because now you're a member of Abraham's family. No one else in your Moabite family will ever enjoy these blessings. God is now in covenant with you because you married a Jew."

And Ruth believed it! With her husband dead, she could return to her Moabite family if she wanted, but to do so would mean forfeiting her place in Abraham's family. She wasn't about to let go of that blessing. Why not? Because she had come into faith. That's why she clung to Naomi—she was clinging to the Abrahamic covenant she had inherited by marrying a Jewish man.

Who instilled this kind of faith in Ruth? Naomi. Naomi's faith was so strong that it altered Ruth's eternal destiny.

Naomi had a contagious faith. When Ruth got infected with that faith, she gained such confidence in Abraham's promises that she turned her back on family, friends, and homeland. This faith was real, and she proved it by refusing to let go of God's covenant mercies.

Naomi demonstrated her faith a second time in the book by returning to the land of Israel. For her, Moab had been a necessary sojourn, but her inheritance was intrinsically bound up in the Promised Land.

KINSMAN-REDEEMER

Then Naomi showed her faith a third time in the book when she said to Ruth, "My daughter, shall I not seek security for you, that it may be well with you?" (Ruth 3:1). Naomi had faith in God's provision for a *kinsman-redeemer* (see Deut 25:5–10). What was a kinsman-redeemer? Briefly, this was the idea:

1. Suppose a married man died prematurely but had no son to carry his legacy.
2. The brother of the dead man was required by Moses' law to marry the widow and give her a son. That boy would be called the son of the deceased man, and the boy would inherit the deceased man's house and property.
3. If there was no brother to perform this duty, a close relative could also perform it. Thus, a *kinsman-redeemer* was a close family relative who restored the dead man's name in Israel by giving him a posterity.
4. The son born to the widow would carry the name of the widow's deceased husband, further his posterity, and provide for the widow (his mother) in her elderly years.

In Naomi's story, Boaz was the kinsman-redeemer. He married Ruth, and Ruth's son became the heir of all that belonged to Naomi's deceased husband Elimelech. The idea of redemption, therefore, is woven throughout Naomi and Ruth's story.

Naomi believed in God's provision through a kinsman-redeemer, and she put her faith to action. She instructed Ruth to go to Boaz (a rich relative) and ask him to serve as Ruth's kinsman-redeemer. When Naomi's faith joined with Ruth's obedience, a very dramatic story unfolded. It ended with Boaz marrying Ruth and then Ruth giving birth to a son named Obed. Obed provided security for Naomi in her elderly years.

"A SON IS BORN TO NAOMI"

When Boaz married Ruth, Ruth bore a son. In response, the women of the city offered their congratulations. But oddly enough, they didn't congratulate Ruth; they congratulated Naomi. Here's what they said to her:

> Blessed be the LORD, who has not left you this day without a close relative; and may his name be famous in Israel! And may he be to you a restorer of life and a nourisher of your old age; for your daughter-in-law, who loves you, who is better to you than seven sons, has borne him (Ruth 4:14–15).

They addressed Naomi because she was the protagonist in the story. Ruth played a pivotal role in giving birth to Obed, but when he was born, he was viewed as belonging to Naomi and propagating her posterity. We see this in Ruth 4:16, "Also the neighbor women gave him a name, saying, 'There is a son born to Naomi.' And they called his name Obed."

Naomi had lost both husband and sons, but Boaz served as a kinsman-redeemer and provided another son for Naomi. The book of Ruth, in a nutshell, tells the story of a mother in Israel who found redemption through the loyalty of her Gentile daughter-in-law.

This is why Naomi's story is a redemption story. Because of a kinsman-redeemer, her losses were redeemed, and she ended her years in security and the promise of an enduring legacy through Obed.

ANTICLIMACTIC?

But wait a minute. Doesn't her redemption strike you as being a little bit anticlimactic? True, the account ends with Naomi holding a baby boy in her arms; but when you consider the significance of everything she lost, getting a baby boy at the end doesn't really seem like a very notable redemption. As already stated, the idea in redemption is that *greater advantages are enjoyed in the end than if the tragedy had never happened.* Did Naomi experience greater advantages in the end?

Well, since Obed inherited his share of Boaz's fortune, Obed provided security for Naomi in her elderly years, and assured her of a posterity. But look at her losses. She had lost both husband and sons. Getting one son back feels more like a consolation prize than a redemption story.

True, getting a son at the end was certainly a comfort to Naomi. That was way better than nothing! But when we consider what redemption stories are supposed to look like, Naomi's redemption feels somewhat anticlimactic. At least that's how it hits me personally. When I consider her grievous losses, the redemption seems to me to be a bit lame.

But wait—the story wasn't over.

REDEMPTION!

For over one hundred years, nobody really paid much attention to Naomi's story. It was almost swept into oblivion by the sands of time. But around one hundred and forty years after Naomi died, when David was established in his kingdom, her story suddenly took on new significance.

I can imagine someone making an appointment and saying to King David, "Your Majesty, are you aware that your great-grandmother had a very unusual story? Have you researched the details on your roots?"

And I can imagine David showing immediate interest: "Investigate that story! I want to know what happened!"

Somebody in David's court went to work and dug up the details. When the full story was pieced together, everyone looked at it and gasped. God had done much more for Naomi than she ever realized! When she died, she had no idea her story was far from over. She didn't know it would unfold like this:

- Obed would beget Jesse, and Jesse would beget David.
- David would become king of Israel and would be given an eternal throne by God.
- David would establish the Davidic Dynasty from which would come the Messiah.

Naomi didn't even realize it, but because of her faith, she gave birth to the Davidic Dynasty! The legacy of her family would include the lineage of the Messiah Himself (see Matt 1:5–6)! Because of her faith, Messiah rumbled right through her tragedy and through her family.

Now, *that's* redemption!

Naomi's story demonstrates that some of Jesus' most glorious purposes are birthed through some of our greatest tragedies. Even Jesus' own tragedy—the cross—gave us a tragedy-to-triumph redemption story.

When David ferreted out Naomi's story, he made it his own. The story found a place in Scripture because of David's ownership. Redemption stories are always meant for the generations. Centuries later, it also became Jesus' story.

Naomi had a redemption story of epic proportions, but when she died, she didn't even know that the best part was yet to be written. Her example reveals a remarkable truth: *Sometimes the fullness of the Lord's redemption in our lives isn't fully realized until after our passing.*

Faith believes in a Redeemer who can write a story that continues to unfold even past our lifetime. Some stories take multiple generations to complete.

What does this mean for you? It means that, if you haven't seen the redemption of God yet, you shouldn't lose heart. When you endure in faith, you keep the story alive. Sometimes you have to stick around long enough to see the salvation of God.

Place your faith in the God of Naomi! Jesus is your Kinsman-Redeemer.

Bereaved three times, Naomi probably viewed Moab as a huge, gaping tomb. But when she stepped into faith, the pangs of her bitter cup became labor pangs that birthed the Davidic Dynasty. Had her husband and sons not died, she would have never received such an astounding legacy. The Lord redeemed her bereavement and turned a tomb into a womb.

FOR SMALL GROUPS

1. Try to read the book of Ruth before your group comes together to discuss this chapter. When you read it as Naomi's story, how does its message change for you?
2. Naomi was depressed (i.e., she used the word *bitter*). Has depression been a fight for you in any way? What has the Lord taught you in your fight with depression?
3. How can we hold to faith even when battling depression?
4. Read Deuteronomy 25:5–10 and talk about the law regarding a
5. kinsman-redeemer. Is there anything about this that you need help to understand? In what way is Jesus our Kinsman-Redeemer?
6. Do you think the author is right, that the story of Naomi would have been mostly buried until the rise of David?
7. *Sometimes the fullness of the Lord's redemption in our lives isn't fully realized until after our passing.* What do you think about that principle? Have you seen it in anyone else's story besides Naomi's?

PRAY TOGETHER

Pray for anyone in the group struggling with depression right now, that their faith might be strengthened.

8

TARGETED

For me, the book of Esther is another book of the Bible with the wrong title. When you open a book entitled *Esther*, you're fully expecting to read the story of a woman named Esther. But even though she's a main character in the plot, it's not really her story. It's Mordecai's story. The heroine is Esther but the protagonist is Mordecai.

Look, for example, at the primary characters in the book. Ahasuerus is mentioned twenty-nine times, Haman and Esther are both mentioned fifty-four times, but Mordecai is named sixty times in the book.

The book of Esther is Mordecai's redemption story. It chronicles his losses and ends with his redemption.

I invite you to revisit the book of Esther but this time read it as Mordecai's story.

MORDECAI'S STORY

The story opens against the backdrop of Ahasuerus, king of Persia, deposing Queen Vashti from her throne. A search is then launched for Vashti's replacement. Esther will end

Targeted

up being that replacement, but even before she's mentioned, Mordecai is placed front and center in the story (Esther 2:5). He's introduced as the man who brought his cousin Esther into his home and "took her as his own daughter" (2:7).

Mordecai's devotion to Esther was so strong that, when she was taken to the palace as a contender to become queen, he paced in front of the court every day to learn of her welfare (2:11). Not long after, the king crowned Esther as queen in place of Vashti (2:17).

The next scene in the book revolved entirely around Mordecai (2:19–23). Overhearing two of the king's eunuchs plotting to hurt the king, he reported the matter to Esther who in turn told the king. The plot was confirmed, and the eunuchs were hung on a gallows.

The next scene in the book once again revolved entirely around Mordecai. Chapter 3 explains why Haman hated Mordecai so fiercely and targeted him for destruction. It was because, when everyone else bowed before Haman, Mordecai refused (3:2). Why would Mordecai not bow to Haman? The reason seems to be linked to their respective ancestries. Haman was an Amalekite and Mordecai a descendant of King Saul's family. Saul had been commissioned by the Lord to utterly destroy the Amalekites for the way they ambushed Israel at the exodus from Egypt (1 Sam 15:1–3), but Saul failed in that mission. Consequently, their respective descendants (Mordecai and Haman) would face each other, centuries later, in yet another great showdown.

When Mordecai refused to bow before him, Haman devised a plot to destroy not just Mordecai, but "all the Jews who were throughout the whole kingdom of Ahasuerus—the people of Mordecai" (3:6). Mordecai was at the bullseye, but Haman's target was the entire Jewish population.

This was Mordecai's tomb. He was staring not only at his own tomb, but that of all his beloved fellow countrymen.

Haman asked the king permission to destroy all the Jews, and offered to fund the entire campaign from his own personal wealth. In response, the king placed all the money and his own signet ring in Haman's hands. With the ring in hand, Haman drafted and authorized a decree against the Jews according to his own pleasure (3:11).

When the couriers went out to proclaim the king's decree to annihilate the Jews, Mordecai knew it was a personal vendetta from Haman. Mordecai felt responsible for the impending death of all his fellow Jews. Putting on sackcloth and ashes, he lifted his voice in a bitter cry (4:1–3). Then he sent a command for Esther to plead to the king on behalf of her people.

ESTHER EMERGES IN THE STORY

Esther and Mordecai exchanged a flurry of written messages, after which Esther agreed to appeal to the king for her people (3:8–17).

Beginning with chapter five, Esther's heroic role in the story really kicks in. Putting her life on the line, she entered the inner court to appeal to the king. When he accepted her by lifting his scepter, she invited him and Haman to a lavish wine banquet. In the meantime, Haman erected a gallows seventy-five feet high so that he might hang Mordecai on it.

Instead of telling the king her request at the first banquet, Esther asked the king and Haman to return the next evening for a second banquet, at which time she would reveal her request.

After the first banquet of wine, the king—in a divinely induced insomnia—couldn't sleep. He called for his chronicles to be read before him, and they read about the time Mordecai had revealed the two eunuchs' plot to harm the king. The king realized he had never thanked or rewarded Mordecai for this kindness, so he decided on the spot to honor him. In a fascinating turn of events, Haman ended up being the one to honor Mordecai. He led Mordecai on horseback through the streets of Shushan and proclaimed before him, "Thus shall it be done to the man whom the king delights to honor!" (6:11).

In chapter seven, Esther held her second banquet of wine for the king and Haman. At that banquet, she revealed her Jewish ethnicity to the king and pled that he defend her people from Haman's plot.

Esther's two-banquet strategy was brilliant. Over and over, she lavished her affection and devotion on the king. She wanted him to be doubly assured of her fidelity and adoration. She was about to show the king his blunder in cosigning with Haman, and if she wasn't careful, the king could feel like this was the Vashti thing happening all over again. But she didn't share Vashti's spirit of accusation. She needed two banquets to doubly assure him of her admiration and trust. With that established, she could cast full blame upon her enemy and say, "The adversary and enemy is this wicked Haman!" (7:6).

In wrath, the king hung Haman on the gallows Haman had prepared for Mordecai.

MORDECAI'S REDEMPTION

In the next verse, Esther introduced Mordecai to the king as her cousin (8:1). Esther and Mordecai teamed together with the king to counteract the evil legislation that Haman had passed. From that day forward, Mordecai worked in the palace and gained increasing favor with the king (9:4).

Esther 9 tells how the Jewish feast of Purim came to be.

In the final chapter of the book, Esther isn't mentioned (10:1–3). Rather, the book ends by describing Mordecai's prominence and greatness. It's a most fitting conclusion to a great redemption story.

By way of review, here are some of the elements that made Mordecai's story a redemption story:

- At the beginning, Mordecai raised Esther in relative serenity.
- The great loss Mordecai suffered was when Haman resolved to kill not only him, but his entire nation.
- The startling reversal of Mordecai's fortunes occurred when the king accepted Esther, granted her request, and overruled the plot to destroy the Jews.
- Did Mordecai enjoy greater advantages in the end than if the trial had never happened? Absolutely! As it says in the concluding verse, "Mordecai the Jew was second to King Ahasuerus, and was great among the Jews and well received by the multitude of his brethren, seeking the good of his people and speaking peace to all his countrymen" (10:3).
- Did the people see the salvation of God? Yes! The Jews watched as God delivered them from Haman's plot of annihilation. They were so overwhelmed by God's salvation that they instituted the annual Feast of Purim. To the present day, they still hold an annual feast to celebrate this great deliverance.

When Haman targeted Mordecai and all the Jews for destruction, Mordecai was staring at one massive tomb. But through faith and intercession, the tomb became a womb that birthed the emancipation of the Jewish nation and Mordecai's international administration.

Mordecai saw a tomb, but God saw a womb!

FOR SMALL GROUPS

1. Try to read the book of Esther before your group comes together to discuss this chapter. When you view the book of Esther as Mordecai's story, how does it change your perspective on the book?
2. The book highlights Haman's hatred of the Jews and his attempt to exterminate them. In what other ways has that same kind of hatred come against the Jews throughout history?
3. In the story, the king gave his signet ring to two men: Haman and Mordecai (3:10; 8:2). How they handled that entrustment is a fascinating study in contrasts. Haman used the ring treacherously to conspire against the Jews and ended up hanging on a gallows; Mordecai used the ring graciously to prosper the king and protect God's people, and ended up being advanced and honored. Do you want to look at the contrast more closely and talk about it?
4. The author wrote about the brilliance of Esther's two-banquet strategy. Do you have any additional insight into why she staged two banquets?
5. Vashti used her stipend to throw a feast for the women (1:9), but Esther used her stipend to throw a feast for the king. In what way does that speak to you?
6. Review the bulleted points at the close of the chapter, about how Mordecai's story was a redemption story. Got any comments about those points? Do you agree that the book of Esther is Mordecai's redemption story?
7. As you've been reading through the book of Esther again, have you seen any other elements in the story that you want to mention as meaningful to you?

PRAY TOGETHER

Pray for the salvation of the people of Israel. The following Scriptures might be helpful launchpads for prayer: Ps 122:6-8; Isa 62:1-7; Rom 10:8; Gen 12:2-3; Ps 25:22; Jer 31:7-14.

9

DETOURED

Caleb was a faith hero in the Bible who faced an unbelievably long detour. He had faith to enter the Promised Land, but instead found himself in a forty-year detour in the wilderness. Let me remind you of the story.

When the people of Israel came from Egypt to the border of the Promised Land, Moses sent twelve spies to search out the land and bring back a report. Caleb and Joshua were two of the twelve.

When the spies returned, ten of them gave an evil report. They said things like, "There's not a chance we can take our Promised Land because it's filled with formidable giants." Caleb and Joshua were the only ones with a good report. They said things like, "God is with us, and with His help we can most certainly take the land."

The nation believed the evil report of the ten, however, and as a consequence, God consigned them to wander in the wilderness for forty years.

That must have been devastating news for Caleb. After all, he had faith to go in, but because the people were unbelieving, he would have to do a forty-year wilderness with all the unbelievers.

Talk about a detour!

I complained to the Lord about that. I was like, "God, that's mean. You really stuck Caleb with a raw deal. It's almost as though it doesn't pay to believe You. I mean, the guy had faith to go in but then got punished with all the complainers because of *their* unbelief."

It's as if God whispered back, "Take another look at the story."

So I examined Caleb's story more closely, and here's what I saw.

AFTER THE FORTY YEARS

After forty years in the wilderness, Israel crossed the Jordan, entered Canaan, and then took five years to subdue the land of Canaan. Once the land was subdued, it was time to subdivide the land and apportion an inheritance to each family. That duty fell to Eleazar the priest and Joshua, Moses' successor.

I can imagine each person coming forward to receive their allotment, and Joshua saying to them, "You get a house in a field." After all, the Canaanites had left behind both furnished houses and cultivated fields for the Israelites to possess.

"Sir, you get a house in a field."

"Ma'am, you get a house in a field."

"Sir, you get a house on a city wall."

"Sir, you get a house in a field."

The land was being distributed equally for everyone to enjoy. And then it was Caleb's turn.

Caleb said, "I don't want a house in a field. I wanted a house in a field forty-five years ago. But if you think I want today what I wanted forty-five years ago, you've got another thing coming."

The wilderness changes what you ask for.

Caleb continued, "I've just come through a forty-year wilderness. I'm talking about a dust-filled, flea-infested, lice-enhanced, scorpion-enriched, serpent-strewn wilderness. I no longer want what I used to want. Now I want more. I want a mountain."

I would have expected someone to speak up, "Who does Caleb think he is, asking for a mountain? The rest of us just got a house in a field. Why should Caleb get a mountain?"

But there's no record that anybody complained about this. It seems that their response was more like, "Caleb wants a mountain? Give him a mountain. He's earned it."

Why were the people willing for Caleb to inherit an entire mountain? Because he had endured the wilderness for forty years. He did the time. The wilderness was where he bought the authority, both with God and man, to ask for—and to take—an entire mountain in the Promised Land.

GOD HAD MORE FOR CALEB

When Caleb first went to spy out the land, I can imagine God looking at him and thinking, *Caleb, I love you. You're My kind of man. I love your faith, your obedience, your passion, your loyalty, your devotion. I want to do something special for you. I want to give you a mountain in the Promised Land. But if I give it to you now, before the wilderness, everyone will complain. They'll think it's unfair, they'll say I'm being partial, and they'll be bitter and indignant toward you. So Caleb, work with Me here. Just do forty years in the wilderness.*

I can almost imagine God shrugging as though it wasn't that big of an ask.

Caleb, just endure for the next forty years in the wilderness. If you'll guard your heart and stay in faith, by the time you come through, you'll have gained the authority with the people to ask for a mountain.

There are some ranks and stations in the kingdom for which you must qualify. You qualify by doing the time. It's the *duration* of your wilderness that qualifies you in the eyes of people.

Someone might look at your wilderness and say to you, "You're in this wilderness because you don't have enough faith." In some cases, that may be true. But in the cases of Caleb and Joshua, they found themselves in a forty-year wilderness *because* of their faith.

The wilderness is the place where you buy spiritual authority. When you endure in faith and do the time, you buy the authority with both God and people to take great mountains for the kingdom of God.

A mountain represents great spiritual enrichment.

More than ever, we need spiritual mothers and fathers who have persevered through the wilderness, done the time, and bought the authority to take mountains. God, give us mothers and fathers who are so abounding in grace that they are rich enough to give an inheritance (as Caleb did) to both sons and daughters.

Pay the price. Do the time. Buy the authority.

When Caleb looked ahead at his upcoming forty-year wilderness, it must have looked like a tomb. "This wilderness is going to kill me! The detour is just too long. In forty years, I'll be dead."

But God was like, "I don't see a tomb."

Caleb's wilderness was actually a womb. That's where he gained the credibility and authority to take a mountain in the grace of God.

FOR SMALL GROUPS

1. Have you ever faced a detour that you thought might kill you? Want to tell the group about it?
2. *The wilderness changes what you ask for.* What does that statement mean to you personally?
3. The wilderness is where we buy authority by doing the time. Do you have any further insight on that idea?
4. *There are some ranks and stations in the kingdom for which you must qualify.* What does that statement really mean for us today?
5. Is there anything else about Caleb's story or the wilderness that you want to talk about?

PRAY TOGETHER

Is there a mountain you're asking God to give you? How can we agree with you in prayer?

10

CRUSHED

When you think *crushed*, the biblical character that comes to mind (besides Jesus) is Job. He was crushed by God in virtually every major area of life: family, livelihood, friendships, and health.

EVERYTHING WAS CRUSHED

Job's *family* was crushed—all ten of his children died in a tornado, and all at the same time. His wife was so distraught by grief that, rather than comforting Job, she pained him further.

Job's *livelihood* was crushed. He raised crops and livestock for a living, but in one day his entire income stream was stripped away. His oxen and donkeys were stolen (they were for crop cultivation), his sheep were destroyed by lightning (they produced wool and meat), and raiders stole his camels (used for trade and transportation).

Furthermore, Job's *friendships* were crushed. In his hour of greatest need, his three best friends turned and persecuted him.

And then his *health* was crushed—he broke out in boils from head to foot. Camping on an ash heap, he took a shard of broken pottery in hand and scraped his sores. Dangling between life and death, it felt like any day could be his last.

TOMB AFTER TOMB

Job didn't simply face a tomb. No, he faced *ten* tombs—the tombs in which he buried his ten children (Job 1:18–19). A closer look, however, reveals that he buried not only his children but also their spouses. (It's reasonable to conclude that if Job 19:17 was pointing to his grandchildren, some if not all of his children were married.) But wait. Look more closely, and you'll see that all his servants were also killed, which multiplies exponentially the number of funerals that overwhelmed the community (1:15–17).

Stop and think about it. How many herdsmen and servants would be needed to service "seven thousand sheep, three thousand camels, five hundred yoke of oxen, five hundred female donkeys, and a very large household" (1:3)? Such a vast estate would require *hundreds* of servants, including men, women, fathers, mothers, sons, and daughters. Since they all perished, the death toll to Job's servant population was *enormous*.

How many women were suddenly widowed? How many children were orphaned? We really don't know. The number of tombs that Job suddenly faced is beyond our ability to calculate. There were more funerals that week than Job could have imagined in his worst nightmare.

It was tomb, after tomb, after tomb.

WHY DID THIS HAPPEN?

Why did such crushing grief hit Job so suddenly? Well, that's the big question of the book. Everyone wanted to know the answer, including Job, his wife, his friends, and his community. The question is so huge that the story surrounding it became the first book of the Bible to be written.[3]

The book of Job is a staged theatrical production. The key players on the stage are Job, his three friends, and a young man named Elihu. Nobody on the stage is given divine information about what has caused Job's calamities. Job gives his best insight as a prophet and man of prayer, and ultimately is the only one who speaks rightly about God (42:8). The other four men debate and speculate based upon the wisdom they've inherited from their ancestors. Through several rounds of debate, these five men duke it out as they bumble their way through circumstances they don't understand—and they're doing it while sitting, unbeknownst to them, before the eyes of the whole world.

We, on the other hand, are in the audience. We're placed by God in the balcony and then handed the entire script. We know the whole story, start to finish. We know what happened in heaven before Job's ordeal, and we know how God will bring it to a climactic and glorious conclusion. We're given *all* the divine information while the players on the platform are given *none*.

Since we have the inside scoop, we just want to talk to the five players as they joust and spar with their arguments. We want to say things like, "Really? You really think that?"

"Stop it! That's nonsense!"

"Aw, come on. You have no basis for saying something like that."

"Job, why are you so depressed? If you knew where God is taking this thing, you would be filled with hope and anticipation!"

"I can't believe you just said that!"

---

1. Most biblical scholars agree that Job probably lived before Abraham, and almost certainly before Moses. When Moses wrote the book of Genesis, therefore, he probably already had the book of Job in his hands.

"You don't *really* believe that, do you?"

"Elihu, buddy, do yourself a favor and shut your trap."

We want to talk to them because we have God's perspective on the entire ordeal.

But then when it's *our* turn—that is, when God puts *us* on the stage, crushes us, and doesn't explain anything about why the trial has happened to us—why do we seem to lose sight of all the wise perspective we had for Job and his friends?

"Yeah, but this time it's different," we say to ourselves. "This time it involves *me*."

When it's our turn, God rarely gives us much divine information, either. And He wonders if we'll learn from all the biblical stories we have in front of us—including Job's. Will we behold and glean from God's faithfulness throughout history, and place our faith in Him to write a redemptive story now that it's *our* turn?

THE STORY IN A NUTSHELL

The book of Job is a fascinating account of how God wrote a redemption story with Job's life. It's an intricate story and more than I can fully tell here. For a more thorough treatment, I suggest my book, *Pain, Perplexity, and Promotion: A Prophetic Interpretation of the Book of Job.* For now, here are the highlights:

God chose his favorite man on earth (Job) to become the first signpost in history to the cross of Christ. That's why his suffering was so intense—it was actually all about the cross.

As one of the oldest books of history, Job's story became the first book in the Bible—that is, the cornerstone of Scripture. Somebody might complain, "You can't build anything on the book of Job." But don't let that throw you off because the builders always reject the cornerstone (Ps 118:22).

God picked a fight with the devil, and Satan responded by wagering a big gamble over Job. Satan basically said, "Job serves

You not because of who You are, but because You bless him. And I'll prove it to You. If You'll remove Your firewall from around him and let me hurt him, I bet he'll curse You to Your face."

God accepted the bet and gave Satan permission to hit Job with incredible calamity. He lost his ten children, all his flocks and herds, and his servants. But instead of cursing God, he worshiped Him (1:20).

But Satan wouldn't concede defeat. He said to God, "You've not really let me touch the man himself. You've only let me touch the stuff around his life. But if You'll remove Your firewall from around His body and let me hurt him in his flesh, that's when You'll really see what's inside the man. You think he's Your friend, but I bet he curses You to Your face!"

God accepted the second bet, and Satan afflicted Job with boils from head to foot. Crawling onto an ash heap, Job curled into a ball of inexplicable pain.

Job's three friends came to comfort him and counsel him on what he should do next.

Their counseling sessions turned into debates on cosmic issues such as sin, righteousness, judgment, the causes of human suffering, and the greatness of God.

Job's friends had a sowing-and-reaping theology. Since Job had reaped punishment from God, he must have sown great wickedness. The issue was sin in his life, and he needed to repent.

Job didn't claim sinlessness, but he insisted that his calamity was not the consequence of sinful compromise. He maintained that he had been living in godly integrity.

Job and his friends went through three full rounds of debates. Then a young man named Elihu went on a six-chapter monologue in which he denounced both Job and his three friends.

Then God came to Job in a whirlwind and grilled him with a litany of questions. Job's answer to every question was the same: *No.* "No, I was not there when that happened. I don't know how such things were made."

Early in the book, Job had called himself blameless (9:21), but later he called himself vile (40:4). He suddenly went from blameless to vile. What caused such a stark switch in his self-assessment? Answer: *He saw God*. When he pivots like that, we just want to ask him, "Job, *what did you see*? What was it that leveled your sense of self-congratulation, and flattened you in utter self-abasement and self-abhorrence?" All I know is, I need the same thing Job needed. I need such a revelation of God that all my self-congratulatory assessments are prostrated in the presence of His majesty and greatness.

Seeing God changed everything for Job. When he prayed for his friends, he was healed. The Lord restored his fortunes, and in the end he had far more than before the trial happened. It was a redemption story!

GOD'S EXPLANATION

When God finally appeared to him, God revealed why Job's trial had taken place.

In chapter 41, God went into an extensive description of a sea creature called Leviathan. From the description, it appears the creature is now extinct, because no sea creature today satisfies the description. The inference is that God chose Leviathan as His illustration because it was the most formidable sea creature of Job's day.

Speaking of Leviathan, God said to Job, "Lay your hand on him; remember the battle—never do it again!" (41:8). In other words, "Job, if you should ever lay your hand on Leviathan, you will never forget the battle, and you'll never do it again. Because he's just that powerful and unconquerable."

Then God went on to say, "Who then is able to stand before Me?" (41:10). In other words, "Job, if you were to lay hold of Leviathan, you would be utterly shaken to the core. How much more now that you've laid hold of the great God of the universe? I'm infinitely more powerful than Leviathan and more fiercely intense than you could possibly comprehend. If you take hold of Me, be prepared for the most confrontive, overwhelming fight of your life!"

God's explanation for Job's ordeal was that *Job had laid hold of Him*. Job had gained God's attention. When Job got God's attention and God turned His gaze on him, Job was utterly crushed. Because God is just that unimaginably powerful.

God had His man caught up in an epic story, and consequently, everyone around him paid a dear price for their association with him—just as with Jesus at His crucifixion.

Through his devotion, Job had placed himself on God's lips. Six times in the book God called him, "My servant Job" (1:8; 2:3; 42:7–8).

What does it take to get your name on God's lips? Many today want their name on the lips of people, but who will labor to get their name on God's lips?

THREE TORNADOES

Let me share my simple outline of the book of Job:

1. Satan's tornado (chapters 1–2)
2. Man's tornado (chapters 3–37)
3. God's tornado (chapters 38–42)

In the first chapter, Satan sent a tornado that killed Job's ten children. That tornado represented Satan's malicious attack against Job.

Next came man's tornado. For thirty-five chapters, Job's three friends and Elihu construed swirling arguments that tore at Job's soul.

But everything changed with the third tornado—when God visited Job and revealed Himself to him (38:1).

Jesus experienced these three tornadoes on the cross. Satan raged against Him, people drove nails into His hands, and the Father forsook Him. Satan, people, God. Those are three big players in the cross and also in our trials.

Have you experienced Satan's tornado in your life? If so, chances are that it was soon followed by man's tornado. But if you've experienced Satan's tornado and man's tornado, is it possible that now you're in line for God's tornado? Wait on the Lord until He comes to you and reveals Himself to you. It'll be worth the wait.

FOR POSTERITY

Redemption stories are always about posterity. Until the next generation owns the story, you haven't yet experienced full redemption.

I wonder if Job was hesitant to write the story. After all, it wasn't exactly complimentary of the other players on the stage. Job's wife, his first set of ten children, his three friends, or Elihu—none of them found heroic status in the book. I can imagine Job not wanting to put the story on paper for the sake of his friends, because they were still his friends and he didn't want to shame them publicly. I'm guessing that he didn't want to expose his wife and friends to dishonor.

If Job was reticent to put his story in ink, we probably have it in written form because of his second set of ten children. By the time the story was finished, his second set of ten children had ownership. I can imagine them saying to their father, "Dad, you *have* to write it! We need it in written form, because *your* story has become *our* story. Give it to us!"

It's likely we have this book because Job's children pressured him to preserve the story for posterity. His children had become stewards of a story, and they felt the responsibility to remember it, honor it, and hand it down to their offspring. When the story was cherished by Job's posterity, it had truly become a redemption story.

The redemption part of the story is what James called "the end intended by the Lord" (James 5:11). God had intended a great and startling turnaround for Job, ending in a face-to-face visitation. God visited Job in glory not because of Job's perfection but in spite of Job's imperfections, for "the Lord is very compassionate and merciful" (James 5:11).

James 5:11 is the interpretive key to the book of Job, showing that God was going somewhere with it. Just as God, in His mercy, had an intended end for Job, He will also be merciful to you and bring you to your intended end.

When the trouble exploded in his life, all Job could see was a massive tomb, but God saw a womb that would birth a redemption story of epic proportions. From the womb of Job's trial has come a story that has empowered every generation ever since, and that to this day keeps turning our eyes back to the cross of Christ.

A TEXAS STORY

Recently, I was speaking at a church in Texas. I expended my voice on the microphone so that, afterwards, I could only communicate with others by writing on a notepad. While unwinding in the green room after the service, I got into a spontaneous conversation with the pastor's wife. It was her first time meeting me, and she was curious about my vocal condition. (At the time of this writing, I'm still limited by a vocal infirmity sustained over thirty years ago.) She asked me, "Is it painful for you when you talk?"

I replied by writing on my notepad, "Every word has hurt for thirty years."

She got this look of heartfelt compassion on her face and softly replied, "I'm sorry."

Here's what I wrote in response: "God has never apologized to me for this."

GOD'S NOT APOLOGIZING

God never apologizes for the trials of life.

He's like, "Job, why should I apologize to you for your horrific trial, when I'm going to make your story the first signpost in human history to the cross of Christ? I'm going to give you the first book of the Bible. I'll give you double your wealth back, and ten more children because of the ten you lost. I'm going to profoundly change you, heal you, and give you a spiritual inheritance in every generation throughout history. Furthermore, I'm going to catch you up in the Spirit, and you will see God *with your eyes*. Why should I apologize to you for this?"

"Joseph, why should I apologize to you for your ten horrific years in an Egyptian prison, when I'm going to use this prison to change everything about you? By the time you come out of this prison, you'll make Pharaoh the richest man on the planet, you'll singlehandedly save the lives of every individual in the nation of Egypt, I'll make you a feeder of *nations*, and your crown jewel—you'll establish your family in prosperity in the land of Goshen. In the womb of Goshen, your family will grow so large that, by the time they come out, they'll be born a nation in a single day. Why should I apologize to you for this?"

"Jesus, why should I apologize to You for Your cross?"

The cross was the most horrific suffering our planet has ever seen, and yet the Father never apologized to Jesus for it.

"Jesus, why should I apologize to You for Your cross, when I'm going to use this cross to gain for You a Bride from every nation and every generation? She will come from every ethnicity, every skin color, every language group, every social strata, every economic class, and every personality type. You will possess her heart, soul, mind, strength, body, finances, time, priorities, and energies. The two of You will be married, and then I'll send You off on an everlasting romantic adventure. Why should I apologize to You for this?"

God never apologizes for the trials of life because, when we see a tomb, He sees a womb.

FOR SMALL GROUPS

1. In what ways do you see the cross in the book of Job?
2. "Job's friends had a sowing-and-reaping theology." It's true that we'll reap what we sow (Gal 6:7). But Job's story shows that, just because someone experiences a fiery trial, it doesn't necessarily mean they've sown sinful behavior. Have you perhaps experienced a trial for which you didn't sow anything sinful?
3. Job went from blameless to vile when he saw God (9:21; 40:4). How would you explain his change?
4. "God's explanation for Job's ordeal was that Job had laid hold of Him." Talk about that statement and its implications for our lives.
5. Talk about the author's three-tornado outline of the Book of Job. How does that help you make sense of the story?
6. What do you think about the author's theory that Job wrote the book because his children demanded it of him?
7. Is there anything else about the Book of Job that you'd like to discuss?

PRAY TOGETHER

Ask God to turn our tomb into a womb. Let's lay hold of God together, just as Job did.

11

SUMMARY

In conclusion, here's a recap of the main points of this book, along with some of the leading sound bites. I'll order them according to the biblical stories we've considered.

1. JESUS CRUCIFIED

    a. On the cross, Jesus went into labor, and at the resurrection the baby was born.

    b. When the disciples looked at the cross, they saw a tomb; when God looked at the cross, He saw a womb (John 16:21).

    c. The agony of the nails brought on the birth pangs that enabled Jesus to push and birth something.

    d. "Give Me My nails, and I'll nail every accusation the accuser uses against you."

    e. Pain can actually become your friend.

    f. There are some things in the kingdom of God you'll never birth until you're in enough pain.

    g. As the firstborn from the dead, Jesus Christ opened the birth canal of resurrection. That was the hard one. Our passage will be much easier.

    h. The seat of the human spirit is in the vicinity of the solar plexus.

    i. Jesus did the cross from His spirit.

    j. The Holy Spirit groans for us only when we engage with Him in groaning.

    k. Feed your Promise, grow it, bring it to full term, push, and birth the thing.

2. ISRAEL ENSLAVED IN EGYPT

    a. God's really good at using famines strategically in our lives.

    b. For over two hundred years, Jacob's family didn't suffer a single casualty to war. They just kept growing.

    c. When Israel came out of the womb of Egypt, they emerged *a nation.*

    d. By the time they came out, they were large enough to enter their Promised Land, take their Promised Land, inhabit their Promised Land, and hold onto their Promised Land.

    e. God puts you into captivity to enlarge you.

    f. Never waste a good prison sentence.

3. JOHN BANISHED TO PATMOS

    a. Isaiah 55:8–9 is God's way of saying, "I agree with you about mostly nothing."

    b. The chasm between John's theology and his experience was agonizingly wide. But still, he got in the Spirit on the Lord's Day.

    c. There is no stopping the man who does his prison from his spirit.

d. Caesar, you might be able to keep John from getting out of your prison, but you can't stop Jesus from getting in.

e. When Jesus teams up with you, the two of you are unstoppable.

f. From the womb of Patmos came the book of Revelation.

g. When you get in the Spirit, you give God room to turn your tomb into a womb.

4. ANNA WIDOWED

a. Redemption stories have several ingredients: initial serenity; deep, agonizing losses; no visible hope of recovery; a startling reversal and vindication; greater advantages enjoyed in the end than if the tragedy had never happened; God glorified.

b. I wonder how often Anna sat and stared at her husband's tomb.

c. "You've taken from me the only thing I've ever asked of You. Who are You, anyway?"

d. "I'm going to pursue You until I see Your goodness."

e. It's not the storms of life that change us, but the pursuit of God *in* the storms of life that changes us.

f. Anna birthed the Messiah through her intercessory ministry. When she held Baby Jesus in her arms, she held the fruit of decades of laborious intercession.

5. ZACHARIAS SILENCED

a. It's tempting, in the face of grueling disappointment, to indulge the flesh and forfeit the inheritance.

b. Zacharias had a life-dominating prayer that preoccupied his mind and dominated his desires.

c. Our prayers linger in God's presence like incense hanging in the air.

d. His physical infirmity felt like a tomb, but Zacharias emerged from it a spiritual father who could raise and rear John the Baptist.

6. JOSEPH IMPRISONED

a. It was prison that put power into Joseph's story and made his a redemption story.

b. God got Joseph into prison, and God got him out.

c. Joseph ended up in prison after doing everything right.

d. Had he kept his eyes on what his brothers did to him, Joseph would have remained a prisoner to their rejection. But because he lifted his eyes to what God was doing in his life, he was liberated to participate in God's purposes.

e. God placed Joseph in a vacuum of fatherlessness to make him a spiritual father.

f. The longer you keep a Joseph buried in prison, the higher he'll rise.

g. Promise trumps prison.

h. A redemption story isn't complete until your posterity carries it.

i. Decide that no one will ever regret giving you privilege.

j. Joseph turned regret into restraint. His restraint made the story.

k. God withholds nothing from us, but He does restrain Himself for strategic purpose.

l. Our restraint gives God room to work.

m. The prison's purpose was to train Joseph to live from his spirit.

n. Joseph became a student of his God language, and that's what got him out. Identify your God language, study it, and master it.

o. Prison is God's accelerated program.

p. Joseph came out of prison with authority over the prison that once held him. Never relent until you clasp in your hand the key to the prison that now holds you.

7. NAOMI BEREAVED

a. The book of Ruth is Naomi's redemption story.

b. Depression is a common response to grief.

c. Even while battling depression, you can grow in faith.

d. Ruth was infected with Naomi's faith.

e. A *kinsman-redeemer* was a close relative who restored a dead man's name in Israel by giving him a posterity.

f. Naomi had lost both husband and sons, but Boaz served as a kinsman-redeemer and provided another son for Naomi.

g. The book of Ruth tells the story of a mother in Israel who found redemption through the loyalty of her Gentile daughter-in-law.

h. After losing both husband and sons, getting one son back feels more like a consolation prize for Naomi than a redemption story.

i. Around one hundred and forty years after her passing, Naomi's redemption took on new significance because of David's rise to the throne. God had done much more for her than she realized during her lifetime.

j. Because of her faith, she birthed the Davidic Dynasty!

k. Had her husband and sons not died, Naomi would have never received such an astounding legacy.

8. MORDECAI TARGETED

a. The book of Esther is Mordecai's redemption story.

b. Mordecai's tomb was Haman's plot to destroy not just him, but all his fellow Jews.

c. Esther arose heroically to appeal to the king to overturn Haman's legislation.

d. Esther's two-banquet strategy was brilliant. She was assuring her husband of her devotion so that, when she showed him he was complicit in approving legislation to destroy the Jews, he would see that she wasn't operating in the spirit of Vashti.

e. Esther and Mordecai worked together to protect the Jews and destroy the enemies of the Jews.

f. In the end, Mordecai was second to the king and ruled the empire with beneficence and peace.

g. Mordecai's tomb became a womb to birth a redemption story.

9. CALEB DETOURED

a. Caleb had faith to enter the Promised Land but instead ended up in a forty-year detour in the wilderness.
b. The wilderness changes what you ask for.
c. In the wilderness, Caleb was buying the authority, both with God and man, to take a mountain in the Promised Land.
d. Caleb found himself in a forty-year wilderness *because* of his faith.
e. There are some ranks and stations in the kingdom for which you must qualify.
f. Pay the price. Do the time. Buy the authority.

10. JOB CRUSHED

a. Job's family, livelihood, friendships, and health were all crushed.
b. Job faced literally *hundreds of tombs.*
c. Five men play out a drama, wondering why Job was crushed by God, but they have no idea why. Then God gives us the whole story in advance, and we watch it play out while having all the divine information.
d. When it's our turn to be crushed, why do we forget all the divine information we've been given on Job and think our situation is bizarrely different?
e. God chose his favorite (Job) to become the first signpost in history to the cross of Christ. The book on Job's life became the cornerstone of Scripture.

f. God and Satan placed bets on how Job would respond.

g. Job insisted that his calamity was not the consequence of sinful compromise in his life.

h. Job went from blameless to vile when he saw God.

i. The Lord restored Job's fortunes, and in the end he had far more than before the trial started. His was a redemption story.

j. Job's trial was so intense because he had laid hold of God.

k. Job's name was on God's lips six times. What does it take to get your name on God's lips?

l. The book is the story of Satan's tornado, man's tornado, and God's tornado.

m. Job wrote the book for his children and their posterity.

n. Job was overwhelmed with all the tombs, but God used the trial as a womb to birth a story that has empowered every generation ever since.

o. God never apologizes for the trials of life because what we thought was a tomb was actually a womb to birth His eternal purposes through our lives.

FOR SMALL GROUPS

1. Review the sound bites in this Summary chapter. Point to the ones that stand out to you, and explain why.
2. Was there a sound bite in the book that really spoke to you, but wasn't mentioned in this Summary?

PRAY TOGETHER

What is your primary takeaway from this study? What are you asking God for? Let's agree together in prayer!

BOOKS BY BOB SORGE

Prayer
Secrets of the Secret Place (paperback & hardcover)
Secrets of the Secret Place: Companion Study Guide
Secrets of the Secret Place: Leader's Manual
Reset: 20 Ways to a Consistent Prayer Life
Unrelenting Prayer
Illegal Prayers
Power of the Blood
Minute Meditations

Worship
Exploring Worship: A Practical Guide to Praise and Worship
Exploring Worship Workbook & Discussion Guide
Glory: When Heaven Invades Earth
Following The River: A Vision for Corporate Worship
Next Wave: Worship in a New Era

Enduring Faith
In His Faith
The Fire of Delayed Answers
The Fire of God's Love
Pain, Perplexity & Promotion: A Prophetic Interpretation of the Book of Job
Opened From the Inside: Taking the Stronghold of Zion
God's Still Writing Your Story
The Chastening of the Lord: The Forgotten Doctrine
The Cross: Never Too Dead for Resurrection
It's Not a Tomb It's a Womb

Leadership
Dealing With the Rejection and Praise of Man
Envy: The Enemy Within
Loyalty: The Reach of the Noble Heart
It's Not Business It's Personal
A Covenant With My Eyes
Stuck: Help for the Troubled Home

For info on each title, go to oasishouse.com.
Call Oasis House at 816-767-8880

Bob's books are also available at:
christianbook.com
amazon.com
Kindle, iBooks, Nook, Google Play
Audible

Stay connected with Bob at:
YouTube.com/bobsorge
Facebook.com/BobSorgeMinistry
Blog: bobsorge.com
Instagram: bob.sorge
Twitter.com/BOBSORGE